Penguin Education

Penguin Modern Economics Texts
General Editor: B. J. McCormick

Political Economy
Editor: K. J. W. Alexander

The Economics of the Common Market
D. Swann

Penguin Modern Economics Texts
General Editor: B. J. McCormick
Senior Lecturer in Economics University of Sheffield

Development Economics
Editor: P. Robson
Professor of Economics
St Salvator's College
University of St Andrews

Econometrics
Editor: G. R. Fisher
Professor of Econometrics
University of Southampton

Economic Thought
Editor: K. J. W. Alexander
Professor of Economics
University of Strathclyde

Industrial Economics
Editor: H. Townsend
Reader in Economics
London School of Economics
and Political Science
University of London

International Economics
Editor: J. Spraos
Professor of Economics
University College London

Labour Economics
Editor: K. J. W. Alexander
Professor of Economics
University of Strathclyde

Macroeconomics
Editor: R. W. Clower
Professor of Economics
Northwestern University
Illinois

Microeconomics
Editor: B. J. McCormick
Senior Lecturer in Economics
University of Sheffield

Political Economy
Editor: K. J. W. Alexander
Professor of Economics
University of Strathclyde

The Economics of
the Common Market

D. Swann

Penguin Books

Penguin Books Ltd, Harmondsworth,
Middlesex, England
Penguin Books Inc., 7110 Ambassador Road,
Baltimore, Md 21207, U.S.A.
Penguin Books Australia Ltd,
Ringwood, Victoria, Australia

First published 1970
Copyright © D. Swann, 1970

Made and printed in Great Britain by
C. Nicholls & Company Ltd
Set in Monotype Times New Roman

Penguin Modern Economics Texts

This volume is one in a series of unit texts designed to reduce the price of knowledge for students of economics in universities and colleges of higher education. The units may be used singly or in combination with other units to form attractive and unusual teaching programmes. The volumes will cover the major teaching areas but they will differ from conventional books in their attempt to chart and explore new directions in economic thinking. The traditional divisions of theory and applied, of positive and normative and of micro and macro will tend to be blurred as authors impose new and arresting ideas on the traditional corpus of economics. Some units will fall into conventional patterns of thought but many will transgress established beliefs.

Penguin Modern Economics Texts are published in units in order to achieve certain objectives. First, a large range of short texts at inexpensive prices gives the teacher flexibility in planning his course and recommending texts for it. Secondly, the pace at which important new work is published requires the project to be adaptable. Our plan allows a unit to be revised or a fresh unit to be added with maximum speed and minimal cost to the reader.

The international range of authorship will, it is hoped, bring out the richness and diversity in economic analysis and thinking.

B. J. MCC.

To Barbara Claire

Contents

Editorial Foreword

Economists are frequently criticized for being 'too theoretical'. Such charges are usually based on a misunderstanding of the methodology of economics, and sometimes on the anxiety of the economists' public to have cut-and-dried answers to practical economic problems. In their defence economists have to point out that the degree of abstraction in economic analysis must be high compared to the complexity of situations in the real world, and that anyway cut-and-dried answers usually rely on chancy assumptions about the future and on value judgements which would not be universally accepted. This defence is particularly relevant in the field of 'political economy', where social judgements, institutional influences, government objectives and economic cause and effect are all relevant but when, nonetheless, it is important to distinguish between them as far as possible. The recent performance and future of the European Economic Community and the consequences of a possible extension of the Community to include the United Kingdom are issues of this sort, clearly in the field of political economy. Indeed the issue of whether to join or not is, for any country faced with it, one of the major and most far-reaching political decisions likely to have to be taken for a generation.

Professor Swann is recognized as one of the few economists in Britain thoroughly informed about the workings of the Common Market, and this text will further enhance his considerable reputation. The book charts a course through the complexities of Common Market institutions and policies, condensing a vast range of knowledge in a way which will be invaluable to the student of economics, the businessman and the general reader. Those who have only a general idea of the workings of the Community will find this an invaluable source-book, filling out the picture in a detailed yet concise manner. The student of economics will note how economic theory is used to explain developments and illumine problems, though the general reader will not find this use of theory obtrusive. The distinction between economics and politics is carefully maintained, yet the economic problems are not considered in a vacuum, but against the background of political objectives and institutional influences. In writing on what is, *par excellence*, an issue in political economy Professor Swann has demonstrated the contribution which economics can make to decision-taking.

K.J.W.A.

Preface

On 25 March 1957, the Governments of France, West Germany, Italy, the Netherlands, Belgium and Luxembourg signed the Rome Treaty. In so doing they agreed to create what is now known as the Common Market or, more accurately, the European Economic Community. The latter title indicates that the arrangement is an economic one although, of course, the political aspect is also of the highest importance. This statement is not likely to give rise to any dispute. A former President of the European Economic Community Commission, Dr Walter Hallstein, once said: 'We are not in business at all; we are in politics.' The political nature of the Community is evidenced by the fact that it has political organs such as the European Parliament and the Council of Ministers. The latter makes binding decisions on matters which were formerly a national prerogative, as in the case of agricultural policy. Moreover, although the Community is primarily concerned with economic integration, the ultimate aim of those who have been in the vanguard of the 'European movement' has always been that close economic ties would eventually lead to political unity.

However, the main burden of this book will be related to the economic aspect of Community policy. This should not be taken as a further indication of the British preoccupation with the economic, as opposed to the political, nature of the 'European movement'. Rather, it is a consequence of the need to achieve some specialization in the analysis of Community policy. Nevertheless, the reader will observe that in the opening chapter frequent reference is made to the political factors which surrounded the creation of the Community. Without an appreciation of the influence of these factors, it would be impossible to understand why Western Europe is divided into two blocs, and why the UK now lies outside the Community.

As the title emphasizes, the focus of attention in this book is the European Economic Community. The more important aspects of policy in the European Coal and Steel Community are also discussed and Euratom is dealt with, although only in passing.

The book has two overriding aims. One is to discuss some of the economic principles underlying the decision to create the Common Market and the policies which the Community has been following since its inception. The second is to discuss the nature of these policies critically. This does not mean that the economic pros and cons of British membership and the prospect of success in joining will be neglected. These topics are in fact discussed at length in chapter 8. It will, of course, be appreciated that many of the subjects treated in this book could be the themes of separate monographs. Because of this, the book seeks to introduce the most important economic features of particular areas of policy, and a reading list is provided for those who wish to delve deeper.

In writing this book I have once more been able to avail myself of the courteous and efficient assistance provided by the London Office of the European Community Information Service. I am greatly indebted to my secretary, Mrs Brenda Moore, who has again rendered a great service by getting the manuscript into a fit state for the publisher.

D.S.

1 The Evolution of the European Economic Community

European Unity in History

Although the actual steps which have been taken to achieve economic and political unity in Europe are mostly, if not all, post-1945 in origin, the idea of such a coming together is not unique to the last quarter of a century. Quite the contrary; history is littered with proposals and arrangements which were designed to foster European unity.

As early as the fourteenth century the idea of a united Christendom prompted Pierre Dubois to propose a European confederation to be governed by a European Council of 'wise, expert, and faithful men'. In the seventeenth century Sully proposed to keep the peace in Europe by means of a European army. In 1693, William Penn, the English Quaker, suggested 'a European Diet, Parliament, or State' in his *Essay towards the Present and Future Peace of Europe*. In the nineteenth century Proudhon was strongly in favour of European federation. He foresaw the twentieth century as opening an era of federations and prophesied disaster if such developments did not occur. It was only after the 1914–18 war that statesmen began to give serious attention to the idea of European unity. Aristide Briand – a Prime Minister of France – declared that part of his political programme was the building of a United States of Europe.

The achievement of a lasting peace has been the chief motivating factor behind the drive for unity. However, economic advantage also played a role. The free trade tradition, and Adam Smith's dictum that 'the division of labour is limited by the extent of the market' was a contributing element. The idea that European nation states were no longer large enough to hold their own in world markets was put forward by the German thinker Friedrich Naumann in 1915.

Despite the fact that there was no shortage of plans to create a united Europe, it was nevertheless not until after 1945 that there occurred a combination of new forces together with an intensification of old ones, which compelled action. In the first place, Europe had been the centre of yet another devastating war arising out of the unbridled ambitions of nation states. Those who sought, and still seek, a united Europe, have always had at the forefront of their minds the desire to prevent any further outbreak of war in Europe. By bringing the nations of Europe closer together it has always been hoped that such a contingency would be rendered unthinkable. The 1939–45 war also left Europe economically exhausted. This engendered the view that if Europe were to recover, it would require a conjoint effort on the part of European states. The war also soon revealed that for a long time Western Europe would have to face not only a powerful and politically alien USSR, but also a group of European states firmly anchored within the Eastern bloc. An exhausted and divided Europe (since the West embraced co-belligerents) presented both a power-vacuum and a temptation to the USSR to fill it. Then again the ending of the war soon revealed that the war-time Allies were in fact divided, with the two major powers – the US and the USSR – confronting each other in a bid for world supremacy. It was therefore not surprising that 'Europeans'[1] should feel the need for a third force – the voice of Europe. The latter would represent the Western European viewpoint and could also act as a bridge between the Eastern and Western extremities.

Europe – The East–West Division

The Economic Commission for Europe (ECE) was one of the first experiments in European regional action. It was set up in Geneva in 1947 as a regional organization of the United Nations (UN), and was to be concerned with initiating and participating in concerted measures aimed at securing the economic reconstruction of Europe. The aim was to create an instrument of co-operation between all the states of Europe, Eastern, Central and Western. Unfortunately, by the time it began to operate, the Cold

1. 'Europeans' – members of the 'European Movement' – sought to break away from systems of inter-governmental co-operation and to create institutions in Europe which would lead to a federal arrangement in which some national sovereignty would be given up.

War had become a reality and the world had been divided into two camps. In the light of future developments in Europe, this was a turning point. Economic co-operation over the whole of Europe was doomed. Thereafter, Western Europe followed its own path of economic and political unity, and Eastern Europe likewise pursued an independent course. This in due course led to two blocs in Europe – the Common Market or European Economic Community (EEC), and the European Free Trade Association (EFTA) on the one hand, and Comecon on the other. Any attempt to build bridges between the Western and Eastern blocs therefore implies trying to break down a division which began to manifest itself in 1947.

The political division of Europe was further revealed in 1948 by the emergence of the Brussels Treaty Organization. The Brussels Treaty was signed by the UK, France, Belgium, the Netherlands and Luxembourg, and was designed to establish a system of mutual assistance in time of attack in Europe. Clearly the Western European states had the USSR and its satellites in mind. This organization in turn took on an Atlantic shape in 1949 when, in order to provide a military defence organization, the North Atlantic Treaty (NATO) was signed by the five states just mentioned, together with the US, Canada, Denmark, Norway, Portugal, Iceland and, significantly, Italy, which had been an Axis power.[1]

Division in Western Europe – The Beginning

The creation of the Organization for European Economic Co-operation (OEEC) in 1948 and the Council of Europe in 1949 marked the beginning of a division between the UK and some of the countries later to become members of the EFTA, and the Six[2] who subsequently founded the EEC.

The division was founded in large measure on the fact that the UK was less committed to Europe as the main area of policy than

1. Greece and Turkey joined in 1952 and West Germany in 1955.
2. The Six are, of course, France, West Germany, Italy, the Netherlands, Belgium and Luxembourg. In discussing divisions between Western and Eastern Europe, and within Western Europe, it should be remembered that the Six were also members of the European Coal and Steel Community (ECSC) and members of the European Atomic Community (Euratom).

the six Continental powers. During the second half of the 1950s the UK was still a world power. She had after all been on the victorious side and had been a major participant to some of the fateful geo-political decision-making meetings such as Yalta. Moreover, she still had the Empire to dispose of. British foreign policy was therefore bound to be based on wide horizons. Relations with Europe had to compete with Commonwealth (and Empire) ties and with the 'special relationship' with the US. In addition, the idea of a politically united Europe (in some eyes the goal was a United States of Europe) was strongly held on the Continent – particularly in France and the Benelux – but, despite the encouraging noises made by Winston Churchill both during the 1939–45 war and after, it was not a concept which excited British hearts.

The difference between British and Continental thinking about the political nature of European institutions was revealed in the discussions and negotiations leading up to the establishment of the OEEC and the Council of Europe.

The war had left Europe devastated. The year of 1947 was particularly bleak. Bad harvests in the previous summer led to rising food prices, whilst the severe winter of 1946–7 led to a fuel crisis. The Continental countries were producing relatively little, and what was produced tended to be retained rather than exported, whilst import needs were booming. Foreign exchange reserves were therefore running out and it was at this point that the US entered upon the scene and the Marshall Plan was proposed. General Marshall proposed that the US make aid available to help the European economy to find its feet and that European governments get together to decide how much assistance was needed. The US did not feel it fitting that it should unilaterally decide on the programmes necessary to achieve this end. Although it seemed possible that this aid programme could be elaborated within the ECE framework, the USSR felt otherwise. Russian reluctance was no doubt based on the fear that if her satellites participated, this would open the door to Western influence.

A conference was therefore convened, and a Committee of European Economic Co-operation (CEEC) was established. The attitude of the US was that the CEEC should not just provide the US with a list of needs. The latter had in mind that the aid it was to give should be linked with progress towards European unification. This is a particularly important point since it indicates that from the very beginning the 'European Movement' has enjoyed the encouragement and support of the US.

The CEEC led in turn to the creation of an aid agency – the OEEC. Here the conflict between Britain and other Western European countries, particularly France, came to a head over the issue of supra-nationalism. France in particular – and she was supported by the US – wanted to inject a supra-national element into the new organization.[1] We should perhaps at this point pause to define what is meant by supra-nationalism. It can refer to a situation in which international administrative institutions exercise power over, for example, the economies of the nation states. Thus the High Authority of the European Coal and Steel Community[2] (the ECSC) was endowed with powers over the economies of the Six and these powers were exercised independently of the Council of Ministers. Alternatively, it can refer to a situation in which ministerial bodies, when taking decisions (to be implemented by international administrations) work on a majority voting system rather than by insisting on unanimity.

The French view was not shared by the British. The latter favoured a body which was under the control of a ministerial council in which decisions should be taken on a unanimity basis. The French on the other hand favoured an arrangement in which an international secretariat would be presided over by a Secretary General who would be empowered to take policy initiatives on major issues. Significantly, the organization which emerged was substantially in line with the UK's wish for a unanimity rule. This was undoubtedly a reflection of the UK's relatively powerful position in Europe at the time. In the light of subsequent events it is also interesting to note that the US encouraged the European countries to consider the creation of a customs union. Although this was of considerable interest to some Continental countries, it did not attract the UK. In the upshot the OEEC Convention

1. It is, of course, ironic that whereas France was then in the vanguard of the supra-national movement she is now its most dedicated opponent.
2. Created under the Paris Treaty of 1951.

merely recorded the intention to continue the study of this proposal. For a variety of reasons, one of which was the opposition of the UK, the matter was not pursued further.

The creation of the Council of Europe also threw into high relief fundamental differences in approach between the countries who later formed the Common Market on the one hand and the British and Scandinavians on the other. The creation of the Council was preceded by the Congress of Europe at the Hague in May 1948. The latter was a grand rally of 'Europeans' which was attended by leading European statesmen including Winston Churchill. The Congress adopted a resolution which called for the giving up of some national sovereignty prior to the accomplishment of economic and political union in Europe. Subsequently a proposal was put forward, with the support of the Belgian and French Governments, calling for the creation of a European Parliamentary Assembly in which resolutions would be passed by majority vote. This was, of course, contrary to the unanimity rule which was then characteristic of international organizations. A Committee of Ministers was to prepare and implement these resolutions. Needless to say, the UK was opposed to this form of supra-nationalism and in the end the British view largely prevailed. The Committee of Ministers, which is the executive organ of the Council of Europe, alone has power of decision and generally decisions are taken on the unanimity principle. The Consultative Assembly which came into existence is a forum – its critics would call it a debating society – and not a European legislature. In short, the British and Scandinavian functionalists, who believed that European unity, in so far as it was to be achieved, was to be attained by inter-governmental co-operation, triumphed over the federalists who sought unity by the more radical method of creating European institutions to which national governments would surrender some of their sovereignty. The final disillusionment of the federalists with the Council of Europe as an instrument of federal unity in Europe was almost certainly marked by the resignation of Paul-Henri Spaak from the Presidency of the Consultative Assembly in 1951.

The Six Set Forth – Success and Failure

The next step in the economic and political unification of Europe was taken without the British and Scandinavians. It took the form of the creation in 1951 of the European Coal and Steel Community by the Six, and this creation marks a parting of the ways in post-war Europe – a parting which by 1959 was to lead to the creation of two trading blocs.

The immediate precipitating factor was the revival of the West German economy. The passage of time, the efforts of the German people and the aid made available by the US all contributed to the recovery of the German economy. Indeed the 'Economic Miracle' was about to unfold. It was recognized that the German economy would have to be allowed to regain its position in the world, and that Allied control of coal and steel under the Internation Ruhr Authority could not last indefinitely. The fundamental question was how the German economy in the sectors of iron, steel and coal (the basic materials of a war effort) could be allowed to reattain its former powerful position without endangering the future peace of Europe. The answer was a French plan, elaborated by Jean Monnet and put forward by Robert Schuman in May 1950. The Schuman Plan was essentially political in character. It sought to end the historic rivalry of France and Germany and to do this by making a war between France and West Germany not only 'unthinkable but materially impossible'. This was to be done in a way which ultimately would have the result of bringing about that 'European federation which is indispensable to peace'. The answer was not to nationalize nor indeed to internationalize the ownership of the means of production in coal, iron and steel, but to create, by the removal of customs duties, quotas and so forth, a common market in these products. Every participant in the common market would have equal access to the products of these industries wherever they might be located, and, to reinforce this, discrimination on grounds of nationality was to be forbidden.

The plan had a number of attractive features. It provided an excellent basis for solving the Saar problem. The handing back of the Saar to West Germany was more likely to be palatable to the

French if West Germany was firmly locked in such a coal and steel community. It was also extremely attractive to the Germans since membership of the Community was a passport to international respectability – it was the best way of speeding up the ending of occupation and of avoiding the imposition of dampers on German economic expansion. It was also attractive to the federalists who had found the OEEC as inadequate to their aspirations as the Council of Europe. The OEEC unanimity rule, and the fact that no powers could be delegated to an independent commission or commissariat, were extremely frustrating. Not only that, but the prospects for the OEEC were not good since by 1952 the four-year period of the Marshall Plan would be over and the UK attitude was that thereafter its budget should be cut and some of its functions passed over to NATO. As it emerged, however, the Community was much more to the federalists' taste since, as already indicated, the High Authority was endowed with substantial direct powers which could be exerted without the prior approval of the Council of Ministers.

The Schuman Plan met with a favourable response from West Germany, France, Italy, the Netherlands, Belgium and Luxembourg. The UK was invited to join but refused. The Prime Minister, Clement Attlee, told the House of Commons:

We on this side are not prepared to accept the principle that the most vital economic forces of this country should be handed over to an authority that is utterly undemocratic and is responsible to nobody (quoted in Palmer *et al.*, 1968, p. 258).

However, the Six were undeterred and in April 1951 the Treaty of Paris was signed. The ECSC was brought into existence and the Community embarked on an experiment in limited economic integration.

The next episode in the development of European unity was also connected with West Germany. When the Korean War broke out in 1950 the response of the US was to suggest that West Germany be rearmed. However, this proposal was opposed by France which was equally opposed to West Germany becoming a member of NATO. However, the French approach to this problem was not a negative one. Instead, the French Prime Minister –

René Pleven – put forward a plan. This envisaged that there would be no German army as such, but there would be a European army to which each participating state, including West Germany, could contribute.

The UK was not opposed to the idea but did not itself wish to be involved. The Six were positively enthusiastic and discussion began in 1951 with a view to creating a European Defence Community (EDC). It was envisaged that there would be a Joint Defence Commission and a Council of Ministers. In addition, there was to be a Parliamentary Assembly and a Court of Justice parallel to those created in connexion with the ECSC. The Six made rapid progress in the negotiations and the EDC Treaty was signed in May 1952.

Having gone so far, there seemed to be a number of good reasons for proceeding yet further. The pooling of defensive and offensive capabilities inevitably reduced the possibility of independent foreign policies. It was therefore logical to follow integration in the field of defence with measures which would serve to achieve political integration was well. Other forces were also at work. One was the desirability of establishing a system whereby effective democratic control could be exercised over the proposed European army. The other was the Dutch desire that progress in the military field should be paralleled by more integration in the economic sphere. The foreign ministers of the Six therefore asked the ECSC Assembly, in conjunction with co-opted members from the Consultative Assembly of the Council of Europe, to study the possibilities of creating a European Political Authority. In 1953 a draft of a European Political Community (EPC) was produced. It proposed that, after a transition period, the institutions of the ECSC and the proposed EDC be subsumed within a new framework. There would then be one European Executive responsible to a European Parliament (the latter would consist of a People's Chamber elected by direct universal suffrage, and a Senate elected by National Parliaments). In addition, there would be one Council of Ministers and one European Court to replace the parallel bodies created under the ECSC and EDC Treaties.

This was undoubtedly a high-watermark in the history of the

'European movement'. The Six had already successfully experimented in limited economic integration in the fields of coal and steel. They had now signed a treaty to integrate defence and were about to go further and create a Community for the purpose of securing political unity. Not only that; the draft treaty proposed to push economic integration still further since it called for the establishment of a general common market based on the free movement of goods and factors of production.

However, on this occasion the success which had attended the Six in the case of coal and steel was not repeated. Five national Parliaments approved the EDC Treaty, but successive French governments felt unable to guarantee success in asking the French Assembly to ratify. Finally, the Mendès-France government attempted to water the Treaty down but failed to persuade the Five. The Treaty as it stood was therefore submitted to the French Assembly. The latter refused to consider it and in so doing killed the EPC also.

An amalgam of motives lay behind the refusal of the French Assembly to consider the Treaty. One was opposition to the supra-national element which it contained. Another was the refusal by the French Left to countenance the rearmament of West Germany and the refusal of the French Right to have the French army placed under foreign control. British aloofness was also a contributory factor. One of the arguments employed by those who were against the Treaty was that France could not take part in the formation of a European army with West Germany if Britain was not a member.

It is perhaps worth noting that the failure of the EDC was followed by a British initiative also aimed at dealing with the problem of rearming West Germany in a way acceptable to the French. A series of agreements were reached in 1954 between the US, UK, Canada and the Six. Under these agreements, the Brussels Treaty Organization was modified and extended. West Germany and Italy were brought in and a new inter-governmental organization – Western European Union (WEU) – was formed. The agreements also related to the termination of the occupation of West Germany and the admission of the latter into NATO. As a counterbalance to the West German army, the UK agreed to maintain specified forces on the Continent. As has been pointed out, the main purpose of the agreement

was to provide a European framework in which Germany could be re-armed and become a member of NATO, while providing also for British military participation to relieve French fears that there would be no check or balance to possible German predominance (Palmer *et al.*, 1968, p. 32).

It should also be noted that the response of Eastern Europe to these agreements was a further hardening of the East–West division in the shape of the formation of the Warsaw Pact.

The *Relance*

Nineteen fifty-four had been a bad year for European unity. The supra-nationalist cause had suffered a reverse and the creation of WEU – an organization cast more in the traditional inter-government mould – had thereafter held the centre of the stage. However, such then was the strength of the 'European movement' that by 1955 new ideas were again being put forward. The re-launching initiative came from the Benelux[1] states. They produced a memorandum calling for the establishment of a general common market and for specific action in the fields of energy and transport. The basic idea behind the Benelux approach was that political unity was likely to prove difficult to achieve. It was the ultimate objective but it was one which could only be realized in the longer run. In the short and medium term the objective should be overall economic integration. Experience gained in working close together would then pave the way for the achievement of the political goal. The memorandum called for the creation of institutions which would enable a European Economic Community to be established. These ideas were considered at the meeting of the foreign ministers of the Six at Messina in June 1955. They met with a favourable response. The six Governments resolved that work should begin with a view to establishing a general common market and an atomic energy pool. Moreover, a committee should be formed which would not merely study the problems involved but should also prepare the texts of the treaties

1. Belgium, the Netherlands and Luxembourg agreed to form a customs union in 1944; it came into effect in 1948 and is called Benelux.

necessary in order to carry out the agreed objectives. An inter-governmental committee, presided over by Paul-Henri Spaak, was therefore created. The Messina resolution recorded that since the UK was a member of WEU and was associated with the ECSC,[1] it should be invited to participate in the work of the committee. The position of other OEEC countries was not so clear – the question of whether they should be allowed to participate was in fact left for later decision by the foreign ministers.

The Spaak committee held its first meeting in July 1955. British representatives were present and then and subsequently played an active part in the deliberations. However, as the committee's probing progressed, differences between the Six and the UK became evident. The latter was in favour of a free trade area arrangement, whilst the Six were agreed upon the formation of a customs union – the Messina resolution had explicitly called for this kind of arrangement. Then again the UK felt that little extra machinery was needed to put the new arrangement into effect. The OEEC, perhaps somewhat strengthened, would suffice. This view was bound to antagonize the federalists who laid stress on the creation of supra-national institutions which would help to achieve more than mere economic integration. These differences culminated in the withdrawal of the UK representatives from the discussions in November 1955. Meanwhile, the Spaak committee forged ahead, although not without internal differences. The French, for example, were anxious about the transition period allowed for tariff disarmament, about escape clauses, about harmonization of social changes and they desired a high tariff round the union whilst the Benelux states were in favour of a low one. In April 1956 the committee reported and its conclusions were considered by the foreign ministers of the Six at Venice in May of that year. Attitudes among the six Governments were not uniform. The French liked the idea of an atomic community, but were cooler on the idea of a general common market. The other Governments held reverse views. However, despite all this, the Governments agreed that the drafting of two Treaties, one to create the general common market and one to create an atomic energy community, should begin. Intensive negotiations followed

1. The UK signed an 'Agreement of Association' with the ECSC in 1954.

and the two Treaties were subsequently signed in Rome on 25 March 1957. These were duly ratified by the national Parliaments. The EEC (and the European Atomic Community) came into being on 1 January 1958.

The Free Trade Area Proposal

As we have seen, at the end of 1955 Britain's attitude towards the Six cooled to such an extent that she withdrew from the Spaak committee. However, as the Six pressed ahead, the UK began to realize that it had severely underestimated the determination which lay behind the *relance*. As a result, a reappraisal of policy took place. In July 1956 the OEEC, under British stimulus, embarked on a study of the proposal that the OEEC states should create a free trade area which would embrace the customs union of the Six. The British hoped that the negotiations for the free trade area, and those relating to the common market, could take place simultaneously, but the Six refused. The OEEC report was completed in December 1956 and published in January 1957. Its conclusions were that a free trade area with the common market as an element was feasible. The UK took this as a signal to take the initiative and proposed that discussions should begin in earnest with a view to creating a European Industrial Free Trade Area. Detailed negotiations on the terms of a Treaty began in March 1957 and continued from October 1957 in an inter-government committee under the chairmanship of Reginald Maudling. These negotiations dragged on until the end of 1958 when they finally broke down.

The negotiations were extremely complex and the reasons for their failure are equally complicated. However, basically the problems were as follows. On the political side, the 'Europeans' were suspicious of the UK's intentions. They suspected that the UK, after it had realized that it had underestimated the impetus behind the *relance*, had decided to take the offensive by proposing a free trade area as a means of wrecking the common market. Furthermore, it was recognized that whilst the path to the achievement of a common market (and what lay beyond) was bound to be hard, a free trade area would confer somewhat similar benefits and yet would involve a relatively less onerous régime. Because of this some members of the Six might lose heart and decide to follow the easier course.

From the economic standpoint the major difficulty was the UK's insistence on a free trade arrangement for industrial goods. Under such a system she would remain autonomous in respect of tariffs on goods emanating from outside the free trade area. This would enable her to go on enjoying her tariff preferences on exports of industrial goods to Commonwealth markets. Agriculture would also be excluded – this was certainly the basis of the earliest British proposals. This left the UK open to the criticism that she wanted the advantage of free access to West European industrial markets without giving a reciprocal concession to Continental food producers. The Commonwealth Preference system also meant that the UK would be guaranteed a continuing supply of food at low world prices. If on the other hand agriculture was brought within the free trade area framework, this low-priced supply of food could be in jeopardy. Indeed, if the agricultural protection systems of the Six were adopted, cheap Commonwealth food would be excluded. The UK would have to buy food at price levels approximating to those paid to farmers in the Six, and the traditional British deficiency payments system would have to be abandoned. It did not escape the attention of the Six that cheap food could have an effect on industrial wages such as to confer an artificial advantage on British industries when competing in the industrial markets of the free trade area.

Another source of difficulty was the degree to which harmonization of such things as social security charges was necessary. The French, particularly, tended to play this up, much as they did in the common market negotiations.

Undoubtedly one of the greatest bones of contention was the problem of the origin of imports and the possibility of deflections of trade. In a customs union, since there is a common tariff level on the imports of, for example, raw materials coming from outside, competitive strength tends to depend on the ability of member-states to transform such inputs into industrial (and agricultural) outputs. In a free trade area, however, member-states are free to decide the tariffs on such imports. These tariffs can therefore differ from state to state and imports of raw materials are therefore likely to be deflected through the low tariff countries. Methods of dealing with this problem gave rise to much technical discussion, but a unanimously acceptable solution was never achieved.

The failure of the negotiations was also in considerable degree due to diplomatic postures, particularly those of the British and the French. The latter left an impression of a certain deviousness. It was difficult to know whether, when they took a stand on a point of principle, it was because they really believed what they said, or whether it was because they found it useful as a means of opposing progress along a particular path. For its part, the UK exhibited some diplomatic weakness. The British undoubtedly underestimated the enthusiasm of the Six for their kind of arrangement. There was a failure to appreciate what the 'Europeans' hoped to achieve in the political sphere. Also there was a tendency to frame our proposals in too stark and provocative a fashion, as, for example, when the UK declared that agriculture should be totally excluded from the free trade arrangement.

The inter-governmental discussion at least served to create an identity of interest between the 'Other Six' – the UK, Norway, Sweden, Denmark, Austria and Switzerland. It was therefore decided early in 1959 that they should press ahead with a free trade area and in this they were encouraged by their industrial federations. Portugal joined the discussions in February 1959 and on 4 January 1960 the Stockholm Convention establishing the EFTA was signed.[1] Western Europe was now divided into two trade blocs.

The EFTA

The EFTA arrangement was one which admirably suited British interests. The institutional machinery is minimal. There is nothing to match the majority voting in the EEC Council of Ministers or the ECSC High Authority's[2] powers of independent action. There are absolutely no signs that the EFTA is a stepping stone to political unity – basically it is a commercial arrangement. The

1. Finland signed an association agreement with the EFTA in 1961.
2. Strictly speaking, this should be in the past tense since in 1967 the commissions of the EEC and Euratom and the ECSC High Authority were merged into one commission located in Brussels.

emphasis is on free trade in industrial goods; in a limited number of cases agricultural goods are treated as industrial goods and therefore tariff reductions have been applied to them. In the main, agriculture is left out of the arrangement, each member being free to decide its own method and degree of support. There is absolutely no question of the agricultural systems of the member-states being organized within the framework of a common agricultural policy. Members are free to determine the level of protection applied to goods coming from outside. This enables the UK to maintain Commonwealth preference not only on industrial but also on agricultural commodities. The latter implies the continuance of a supply of cheap food and the deficiency payments system of agricultural support.

Two features of the EFTA arrangement deserve special mention. One is that because of differences in national tariffs on goods coming from without, it has been necessary to elaborate origin rules and a customs procedure so as to determine whether goods can be accorded the full benefit of the EFTA tariff reductions. The other is that the EFTA Convention makes few demands on members in the field of harmonization of taxation, social security charges and the like.

Reappraisal and Entry Bids

The ink of the Stockholm Convention had not long been dry before the UK began a major reappraisal of policy. As late as 1959 leading British Ministers went on record as saying that for a variety of reasons – our Commonwealth ties, the British agricultural support system, doubts about supra-nationalism – the UK could never contemplate joining the EEC. However, it is clear that from 1960 a reappraisal of policy was under way. By 1961 the re-thinking had proceeded far enough for the Prime Minister – Harold Macmillan – to announce that the UK intended to apply for membership of the EEC and for its part would be willing to join provided the special needs of the UK, the Commonwealth and the EFTA could be accommodated. The failure of this attempt, and that of Harold Wilson in 1967 together with the renewed prospect of negotiations in 1970, are recorded here merely to complete the story.

2 Tariff Barriers and the Customs Union

Within the EEC the free movement of goods has been stimulated by the action taken to dismantle tariffs and quota barriers and by attacks on those factors, non-tariff in character, which either prevent or distort intra-Community trade. In this chapter the focus of attention will be on those aspects of Community policy which relate to tariffs and quotas.

Forms of Economic Integration

Economic integration can take many forms and these can be ranged in a spectrum in which the degree of involvement of participating economies, one with another, becomes greater and greater. The *free trade area* is the least onerous in terms of involvement. It consists of an arrangement between states by which they agree to remove all customs duties (and quotas) on trade passing between themselves. Each party is free, however, to unilaterally determine the level of customs duty on imports coming from outside the area. The proposal put forward by the UK in 1957 typified such an arrangement, although it will be remembered that the initial British proposal related to industrial goods only and was therefore rather narrow in conception. The EFTA is of course an example of such an industrial arrangement actually in operation although, as noted in the previous chapter, some agricultural goods have been treated as industrial goods and accorded tariff reductions under the Stockholm Convention.

The main problem of the free trade area is connected with the origin of goods. Since parties can apply differing rates of customs duty on goods coming from without, certain problems arise. Suppose, for example, that area member A applies a zero import duty whilst area member B applies a duty of 20 per cent. An exporter in a non-member country wishing to send goods to country B will probably route them through country A. We say 'probably' because it will only pay to do so if the saving in import duty more than offsets any extra freight and handling costs arising from the deflection of trade through country A. There are a number of features of such a situation which are worth highlighting. Firstly, the non-member countries' goods will not only enjoy tariff-free treatment on entry into country A but (provided the free trade arrangement is fully operational) will benefit from the tariff free entry into country B accorded under the free trade agreement. But the non-member will not necessarily have given country B any reciprocal trading concession. In effect country B's tariff has been undermined. Secondly, the deflection of goods through country A enhances the latter's prosperity at the expense of country B. Thus, if the import duty into country A was not zero, country A could raise extra revenue at country B's expense. Furthermore, country A will be able to develop extra freight and handling business out of the deflection of trade through its ports. Then again producers in country A who incorporate the imported goods into their exports to the rest of the free trade area would be at a competitive advantage as compared with similar producers in country B.

When drafting the Stockholm Convention the EFTA countries had therefore to devise origin rules which would enable the customs authorities to determine which particular goods could be accorded the advantage of tariff elimination. Such tariff treatment is granted if the goods are deemed to be of 'area origin'. The latter applies if they meet any of three criteria. Firstly, the goods in question have been wholly produced within the area of the Association. This is a most obvious criterion although in practice it is not always applicable to manufactured goods. It has been pointed out that

in order to qualify under this criterion, goods must have been produced in the Area entirely from materials, parts or components which themselves are shown to have been 'wholly produced' in the Area. The use of any materials, parts or components, however minor, of non-EFTA or undetermined origin is sufficient to prevent a product from satisfying this criterion (EFTA, 1966, p. 76).

Secondly, the goods have been produced within the area of the Association and the value of the materials imported from the countries outside the area (or of undetermined origin) which have been used in their production does not exceed 50 per cent of their f.o.b. export price. The latter is called the 'percentage criterion'. Thirdly, the goods have been produced by a specified process of transformation. This is termed the 'process criterion'.

The next stage in economic integration is the *customs union*. Here tariffs and quotas on trade between members are removed but members agree to apply a common level of tariff on goods entering the union from without. Because of the latter factor, rules of origin are unnecessary. Article 9 of the Rome Treaty declares that the Community shall be founded upon a customs union, but in fact the Community is more than just that. It is indeed referred to as a *common market* and the latter technical term implies that the free movement of factors of production – labour, capital and enterprise – exists alongside the customs union. This is in fact the case in the EEC, but the term 'common market' is still an inadequate description of the economic arrangement envisaged by the Rome Treaty. The latter calls for common policies in agriculture and transport and harmonization of policy in fiscal and other fields. These requirements push the Community beyond the level of a common market and in the direction of an *economic union*. There are of course degrees of economic unification. We could envisage as an ultimate stage a situation in which there were common policies on all economic matters as well as a common currency – all operated presumably under a supra-national authority. Clearly the Rome Treaty does not call for such a high degree of economic unity.

The Basic Theory of a Customs Union

We have seen that although in terms of economic integration the Community tends towards an economic union, its tariff and quota policy is based upon the creation of a customs union. It is therefore appropriate to consider what economic theory has to say about customs unions. Present understanding of the theoretical implications of such arrangements is based on the pioneer study of the subject by Professor Jacob Viner. The issues involved were subsequently developed by Professor James Meade and others. What follows is an elementary analysis based on Meade's basic theoretical formulation.

Static analysis: production effects

An important point which emerges is that the advantages of trade liberalization within the framework of such a union need to be kept in perspective. Customs unions *per se* are not so unambiguously beneficial as is universal free trade. Classical economists, such as David Ricardo, were able to demonstrate theoretically that the universal elimination of protection, particularly if it was at a high level, would lead to a great increase in world welfare. Each country would specialize in the production of those goods for which it was best fitted – in economists' language, countries would specialize in producing those goods in respect of which they have a comparative advantage. Taking the world as a whole, greater production would result than if countries insisted on protecting their industries and producing all or most of the goods which they needed. (The division of the increase of production would, of course, depend on the terms of trade.) But a customs union is not so unambiguously beneficial because it is not in effect universal – it represents free trade within a bloc and discrimination against the rest of the world. Thus in appraising the results of a customs union, two effects have to be distinguished. One is trade creation, which represents an improvement in resource utilization, and the other is trade diversion, which represents a deterioration. These two effects are illustrated in Table 1. We assume the following:

1. The world consists of two countries, I and II, who wish to form a customs union, and a third outside country which we term country III.

2. Only three commodities are produced – A, B and C.

3. Prior to the customs union country I applied a 50 per cent *ad valorem* tariff to all imports, but after the formation of the union the tariff only applies to imports from country III.

Taking good A first, the lowest-cost producer is country III which lies outside the proposed union. Before the union, good A produced by country III (with duty applied) undersells A produced by country I, or A produced by country II (with duty applied). But after the union is created, A produced in country II

Table I

Trade Creation and Trade Diversion (£)

Good	Cost or cost plus duty per unit	Country III exporting to country I	Flow of trade	Goods produced by country I	Flow of trade	Country II exporting to country I	Results
A	Cost	12		20		14	Trade diversion
	Cost plus duty prior to customs union	18	→	20	No trade	21	
	Cost plus duty after customs union	18	No trade	20	←	14	
B	Cost	14	No trade: country I produces B	17	No trade: country I produces B	12	Trade creation
	Cost plus duty prior to customs union	21	No trade	17		18	
	Cost plus duty after customs union	21	No trade	17	←	12	
C	Cost	16	No trade	10	No trade	12	Neither trade creation nor trade diversion. Country I is the lowest-cost producer and provides C before and after the union
	Cost plus duty prior to customs union	24	No trade	10	No trade	18	
	Cost plus duty after customs union	24	No trade	10	No trade	12	

no longer has duty applied to it and as a result undersells A produced in country III (bearing duty) and A produced in country I. This is called trade diversion. In the case of good B the lowest-cost producer is country II. But even prior to the union B produced in country II does not enter country I. This arises because the customs duty renders B produced in country II uncompetitive with B produced in country I. But after the union is created B produced in country II no longer has a customs duty applied and it enters country I and undersells B produced in country I. Here we have trade creation. In the case of good C, the lowest-cost producer is country I. It produces the good before and after the union. As a result neither trade diversion nor trade creation occurs.

It follows that in assessing the effects of a customs union we have to take into account that it can shift production away from the lowest-cost producer to a higher-cost member of the union. Such trade diversion is a departure from a previously more rational pattern of resource allocation. On the other hand, the creation of the union can shift production away from a less efficient to a more efficient member of the union and such trade creation represents a shift towards a more economic pattern of resource allocation. As a first approximation, therefore, we can conclude that whether or not a customs union is beneficial depends on the balance of these two effects.

How can the balancing be carried out? In the case of good A in Table 1, suppose that country I imports one million units first from country III and then from country II. The original cost was therefore £12 million but is now £14 million. The cost of trade diversion – the extra cost incurred by virtue of obtaining supplies from the higher-cost source – is therefore £2 million. In the case of good B, suppose country I consumes half a million units; then the saving of trade creation is £2·5 million. On balance therefore, taking account of production effects only, the customs union is beneficial.[1]

This analysis is, however, based upon a number of simplifying assumptions. The first is that the demand for the goods in question is totally inelastic. This simplifies matters since in calculating the

1. We can ignore good C since there was no change from pre- to post-union.

gains and losses we can assume that any changes in the price of A or B which result from the formation of a union will not cause the quantities consumed in country I, pre- and post-union, to differ. The second assumption is that supply curves are infinitely elastic. Clearly the absence of such an assumption would complicate the calculation of gains and losses since costs will change with movements along supply curves. It follows from all this that a union can have both advantageous and disadvantageous effects. Whether it is beneficial or not depends on the balance of the effects of trade expansion and contraction.

One thing is clear: the static analysis of customs unions does not of itself provide a basis for categorically commending or rejecting them. Whether they are good or bad depends upon the particular circumstances. However, some generalizations do emerge although it must be admitted that there is no substitute for measurement in deciding the actual results of a union. Firstly, a customs union is more likely to be advantageous on balance if the economies of the partners are actually very competitive but are potentially complementary. If they produce similar products but efficiencies differ, they will each contract their relatively inefficient industries and expand their efficient ones. There will be a beneficial increase in mutual trade without much diversion of imports or exports from other markets. If, on the other hand, their economies are already complementary, the prospects of gains on the production side would be correspondingly small. Secondly, a customs union is more likely to increase economic welfare the higher the initial duties on imports from partners. High duties imply high levels of inefficiency which are being protected. Thus the higher the inefficiencies the greater the gains from trade after such protection is removed. Thirdly, the production effects of a customs union will be the more advantageous the lower its tariff against the outside world. Fourthly, a union is more likely to raise welfare the greater the proportion of world production, consumption, and trade covered by it. The larger the union becomes the greater the probability that trade creation will outweigh trade diversion, until, in the case of a union embracing the world, trade diversion ceases to exist.

Theoretical assessments

Predictions based on economic models reveal that the benefits of Western European customs unions are not great. Most of the studies which have been undertaken agree about one thing and that is that the gains are very small indeed – as little as 1 per cent of Community GNP. Why is the beneficial effect so limited? One answer is that a rather small part of total production is traded internationally. Thus services, building and much of the purchases of the public sector do not enter into international trade and the net gain from customs unions can only arise in connexion with that part of production which is traded. Secondly, as has been pointed out by Nils Lundgren (1969), if the removal of protection is to be significant it must have been costly to maintain. However, examples of really costly protection are rare since there is no great political support for such protection. For example, raw materials are normally duty free, largely because the production of them at home would involve astronomic costs. Much the same is true of more specialized commodities such as ships and aircraft. It is important to stress that we are not implying that the gains from international trade are small. On the contrary, because of the uneven geographical distribution of natural resources and so forth, they are enormous. But the fact is that these gains are already being substantially reaped since no one can afford not to reap them, and the existence of a substantial volume of international trade is a proof of this fact. As a consequence further gains from customs unions are bound to be limited.

Dynamic analysis

We may therefore legitimately ask why so much emphasis is placed on the creation of customs unions. The answer is partly political in that the process of economic integration prepares the ground for political unification. But the other reason is that the trade creation – trade diversion analysis of customs unions ignores many of the other advantages which can accrue to the participants. Firstly, a larger market gives rise to opportunities for the fuller exploitation of economies of large-scale production.

National markets may not be big enough to enable firms to expand sufficiently to achieve the minimum optimal scale, and such a scale of plant or firm may require the sales area of the much larger Community market. The much bigger Community market may also enable firms to expand and thus mount the research and development efforts which are necessary if European firms are to compete successfully with their American rivals. Secondly, there are some reasons for believing that the intensity of competition may increase as a result of the formation of a union. For example, industrial structures undergo a change. National monopolies become Community oligopolies and the situation in established oligopolies becomes more fluid, with a reduction of oligopolistic collusion and mutual awareness. Then again there is a possibility of a psychological change. Thus it has been argued that prior to the formation of the EEC relations between competitors in the relatively small national markets were personal and friendly. Competition manifests itself in the attempt of producers to expand at each other's expense. This was unlikely to happen under such circumstances. However, when trade liberalization occurred firms in one national market could seek to grow not at each other's expense but at the expense of producers in other national markets with whom relations are impersonal. Not only that but producers in those other markets would tend to behave likewise. As a result every firm would become aware of the fact that its own national market share could no longer be regarded as secure. Because of this they would tend to look less favourably on the preservation of less efficient compatriots. Of course, the much more aggressive business behaviour which now exists in the Community is due not only to the opening up of markets, but also to the infiltration of US investment which has brought with it more aggressive business strategies and better management techniques. But this infiltration was undoubtedly to a considerable degree the result of the bigger market, or the prospect thereof, which the Rome Treaty opened up, and is in effect another advantage of the customs union from the point of view of the members. Thirdly, although it is not strictly speaking a dynamic advantage of a customs union, it is necessary to point out that such an arrangement is likely to enable the members to extract better terms when they bargain together in, for example, international negotiations such as the Kennedy Round.

Tariff Disarmament and Trade Expansion

The Rome Treaty requires that internal tariffs be eliminated. As we have seen the French, particularly, were anxious about the transition period allowed for tariff disarmament to be accomplished. In the up-shot it was decided that the period should be one of twelve years so that all tariffs would have to be eliminated by 31 December 1969. Table 2 shows a progress in tariff reduction on industrial goods and also indicates that the Community accomplished its tariff disarmament ahead of schedule. The Treaty also called for the abolition of quotas and this has been achieved, although the task was rendered relatively easy by virtue of measures of liberalization accomplished within the framework of the Internal Monetary Fund (IMF), the General Agreement on Tariffs and Trade (GATT) and above all the OEEC, prior to the coming into operation of the Rome Treaty.

This liberalization has been accomplished with relatively little trouble. We may well ask why this is so, particularly when we consider that countries are generally rather concerned about the level of their protection. The answer in some degree must be the obvious one that the liberalization process has been reciprocal. Then again too much should not be made of the idea that, because of differences in efficiency between states, the competitive process will lead to the absolute contraction or closing down of some enterprises. During a period of rapid expansion, such as has been experienced by the Six since 1958, it is more likely that competition will result in a smaller share of the overall development going to the less efficient and a larger share to the more efficient. There have however been some problems. For example, Italian kitchen equipment has caused considerable havoc in the French industry and led at one stage to the temporary levying of a tax on imports of Italian refrigerators. Mergers occurred in order to obtain the economies of large-scale production and to eliminate excess capacity. The other main occasion when anti-liberalization measures were introduced was 1968 when the French government

Table 2

Internal Tariff Reductions of the EEC (Per Cent)

	1.1.59	1.7.60	Acceleration of 1.1.61	1.1.62	Acceleration of 1.7.62	1.7.63	1.1.65	1.1.66	1.7.67	1.7.68
Individual reductions made on 1 January 1957 level	10	10	10	10	10	10	10	10	5	15
Cumulative reduction	10	20	30	40	50	60	70	80	85	100

Source: EEC Commission (1967), p. 34.

imposed quotas on French imports. However, this measure did not stem from the disturbances caused by trade liberalization but from internal political unrest. The quotas were approved by the EEC Commission, although after the event.

Simultaneously with the elimination of internal tariffs, the Community erected a common external tariff. According to the Treaty the external tariff was to be equal to the unweighted arithmetical average of the duties on imports from third countries which were operative on 1 January 1957. The annexes to the Treaty do, however, contain exceptions to this rule. For example, list B includes eighty commodities, mostly raw materials, with respect to which the common tariff is not to exceed 3 per cent. Table 3 shows how the Community progressed towards the establishment of the common tariff.

Table 3

The Creation of the Common External Tariff (Per Cent)

	Acceleration of 1.1.61	1.1.62	Acceleration of 1.7.63	1.1.66	1.7.68
Industrial products					
adjustment	30		30		40
cumulative adjustment	30		60		100
Agricultural products					
adjustment		30		30	40
cumulative adjustment		30		60	100

Source: EEC Commission (1967), p. 34.

The liberalization of trade within the Community has naturally given a considerable fillip to intra-Community trading. There has also been an increase in the rate of expansion of the Community's imports from third countries, though of modest proportions by comparison. The contrast between the rate of expansion of intra-Community trade and trade with third countries is high-lighted by the fact that, taking the time periods 1953–8 and 1958–67, whilst the average annual percentage increase in imports from third countries rose from 9·4 to 10·0 respectively, intra-Community trade increased from 14·2 to 28·4.

The Creation of the EFTA

More or less simultaneously with the liberalization within the EEC, the members of the EFTA created the free trade area. Table 4 indicates the progress of tariff disarmament and shows that the EFTA too was able to achieve an acceleration of liberalization. It should, however, be noted that two member-states – Portugal and Finland – enjoy the advantage of a slower rate of reduction of their import duties. Portugal was given until 1980 to remove its duties entirely and Finland until the end of 1969.

Table 4

Tariff Disarmament in the EFTA

	Original timetable EFTA rate as % of basic duty	Date	Actual timetable EFTA rate as % of basic duty	Date
	80	1.7.60	80	1.7.60
	70	1.1.62	70	1.7.61
General timetable	60	1.7.63	60	1.3.62
under Article 3	50	1.1.65	50	31.10.62
of the	40	1.1.66	40	31.12.63
Stockholm	30	1.1.67	30	31.12.64
Convention	20	1.1.68	20	31.12.65
	10	1.1.69	0	31.12.66
	0	1.1.70		

Source: EFTA (1966), p. 59.

With regard to the growth of intra-EFTA trade and EFTA trade with the rest of the world, a number of features are worthy of attention. Firstly, the average annual percentage increase in intra-EFTA trade between 1959 and 1967 was nearly three times as great as the rate of increase between 1953 and 1959. This compares favourably with the approximate doubling over a more or less similar period of time in the case of the EEC. On the other hand, the actual annual rate of increase since the beginning of tariff disarmament is significantly slower in the EFTA than in the

EEC. The average annual rate of increase of trade with the rest of the world since the beginning of tariff cutting has been faster than before it, and this is more marked in the EFTA than the EEC. The average annual rate of increase of trade with the rest of the world is, however, faster in the EEC than in the EFTA.

3 Non-Tariff Barriers

Although it is difficult to quantify the significance of non-tariff barriers in relation to the free movement of goods, there is good evidence, qualitative rather than quantitative, which suggests that they consitute a powerful factor preventing and distorting intra-Community trade.

Indirect Taxes

Indirect taxes in the Community are of two kinds – turnover taxes and excise duties. Within the general category of turnover tax the Community has operated two main kinds – the cascade and the value added systems. The latter is known as the *la taxe sur valeur ajoutée*, or TVA. Until quite recently all the member-states except France employed the cascade system and we will discuss this first.

The cascade tax is a multi-stage tax in that it is levied at each stage of the productive process. In practice it has covered a broad range of products. It is therefore unlike the British purchase tax, which is a single-stage tax levied at the level of the wholesaler, and which covers a relatively narrower range of goods. Cascade taxes are levied on the gross value of output at each stage in the chain of production. The important point to note is the cumulative nature of the system. Tax is applied at each stage upon the whole selling value including tax. If the product is used in further production, the selling price of the resulting product upon which tax is charged will be inflated by tax paid at the previous stage. Under the cascade system the cost of producing a given product excluding tax (that is, the value added) may be the same whether produced by a vertically integrated firm or by a vertical series of independent enterprises, but the tax paid on the product of the latter will be greater than that levied on the former.

The French have, however, favoured the TVA. Basically the principle of this type of tax is that it is paid at each stage in the process of production upon the value added at each point in the productive chain. The final price of the product, in the absence of turnover tax, is equal to the sum of the values added at each point. Because of this fact it makes no difference whether the tax is collected at several points or as a single payment on the final product. The tax collected will be the same in either case – the tax is therefore neutral as between production which is carried out in a vertically integrated firm and production which is carried out by several separate firms with tax levied at the intermediate stages.

Before we can appreciate how the operation of the cascade system distorts intra-Community trade, it is necessary to draw attention to the treatment of indirect taxes in international trade. Generally speaking, when a good is exported from the country of origin any indirect tax levied on the good is reimbursed. When it arrives in the country of destination a countervailing duty, equal to the indirect tax in the country of destination, is imposed. This is known as the destination principle. It contrasts with the origin principle which implies that a good bears the indirect tax levied in the country of origin and if exported continues to bear it. Under the latter system there is no need to reimburse taxes or apply countervailing duties.

With this distinction in mind, it is not difficult to see how, in practice, a combination of a cascade tax and the destination principle can distort intra-Community trade. This arises from the fact that it is sometimes extremely difficult to know just how much tax a good bears and therefore how much tax ought to be reimbursed upon exportation. Therefore, the possibility exists that unintentionally an unduly large rebate may be given; it is equally possible that such an unduly large rebate may be given intentionally. In other words, the fiscal system could be used to confer upon home producers an artifical advantage in the export market.

But there are other reasons for a change of system. From what has gone before it is evident that the cascade system gives an artificial incentive to vertical integration. This has several disadvantageous effects. Firstly, it may be more efficient to specialize in one stage of a productive process, but the tax discourages this. There may, of course, be no advantage as between vertically integrated and non-vertically integrated firms from the point of view of productive efficiency. But the vertically integrated firm enjoys an artificial competitive advantage. Secondly, although from the view of maintaining competition it is usual to regard horizontal concentration as a main problem, there are reasons for fearing the vertical variety. A firm which is integrated backwards can control supplies of raw materials and semi-finished products to competitors and force them out of business or to conform to its wishes. However, this problem only arises if firms at an earlier stage in the production process are concentrated horizontally, and this is not inevitable since the tax does not bias industrial structures in this way. But it could be argued that by integrating vertically an enterprise could acquire financial resources which would enable it to concentrate horizontally. Such resources would enable it to endure the price wars which might be necessary to discipline non-vertically integrated firms. Thirdly, it should be pointed out that there are reasons for believing that vertical integration in industry tends to impede cross-frontier competition. This argument is based on the proposition that in the absence of such integration firms at any stage of production have the alternative of buying the products of the previous stage either from domestic enterprises or from foreign firms. In effect an import gap exists. With vertical integration this possibility does not exist.

There are two other arguments favouring a change in the Community's tax structure. One is that in creating the Common Market the aim has been to produce within the enlarged market of the Six conditions which are analogous to those existing in a national market. But the destination principle means that the administrative procedures for reimbursing indirect taxes and applying countervailing duties must be maintained and this constitutes a fiscal frontier not normally present when goods flow within national boundaries. The other argument relates to the obvious fact that a common market can hardly be said to exist when consumers in the various member-states pay different prices for the same goods because national tax rates differ.

Article 99 of the Rome Treaty requires the Commission to make proposals which will enable national turnover taxes to be harmonized in a way which contributes towards achievement of the goals set by the Treaty. The Community's response to this requirement is contained in two directives which were adopted by the Council of Ministers in April 1967. The first required that a common system on the value-added model be adopted by all the countries by 1 January 1970. This represents a shift towards the French system although the French tax will have to be brought into line with the European TVA. This will deal with two problems. Firstly, the incentive to further vertical integration will be eliminated. It is important to stress the word 'further' since it is not likely that the vertical integration already in existence will be reversed. The latter is only likely if vertical integration is downright uneconomic and has only been worth-while because of the tax advantage. This attack on vertical integration will also help to prevent the plugging of import gaps. Secondly, since it is easier in the case of a value-added system to assess the amount of tax which a good bears, it will be less easy to use reimbursements and countervailing duties as a means of distorting and inhibiting intra-Community trade.

The second directive concerns the detailed operation of the European TVA. The common tax is to be a general one, levied in principle at each stage of the economic process in such a way that it falls on the value added at each point. The Neumark Committee, which was set up in 1960 to deliberate on fiscal problems relating to the establishment of the Common Market, suggested that the tax should only extend up to the wholesale stage and that a separate tax should be levied at the retail level. This proposal was based on the idea that the level of the retail tax would be variable and could therefore be used to compensate individual states for any disturbance of indirect tax revenue caused by harmonization. This suggestion has been adopted to the extent that, up to the time when national rates are harmonized and fiscal frontiers abolished, member states can limit the field of application of the tax up to and including the wholesale stage. Services will be taxed if they have a marked direct or indirect effect on the price of goods. A list of such services has been drawn up and it includes freight transport. Banking has been excluded.

The second stage in the harmonization process is the equalization of national rates. The Council of Ministers will have attempted to make such a decision, on a proposal of the Commission, by 1 January 1970, when the common structure comes into effect. When common rates are established, the Six will shift to the origin system. By so doing the Community will eliminate the need for tax reimbursements and countervailing duties, and will therefore further prevent the distortions and inhibitions to which they give rise. The fiscal frontier as a psychological factor (and a costly administrative procedure) will be eliminated. The Common Market will also be more of a reality in that prices of particular goods will *tend* to equality over the whole territory of the Community.

We turn now to the problem of excise duties which as a revenue raiser are relatively less important in the Community than in the UK. These, too, create a problem since the practice of various member-states is not uniform in respect both of what goods they levy such duties on and the rates levied. Given such a situation, the question arises should the Community choose the origin or the destination system? Suppose it chooses the former. Let us consider two countries which we may designate I and II. Let us assume that they both produce two goods, X and Y. Suppose country I decides to levy a high excise duty on good X and country II decides to levy a high excise duty on good Y. Country I would find sales of X falling off both at home and in country II. Country II could find sales of Y falling both at home and in country I. Sales of Y produced by country I and sales of X produced by country II would expand, although this development would not reflect their factor endowments but would be due to fiscal factors. A shift to the destination principle would solve the problem. It would, however, give rise to a fiscal frontier. The Neumark Committee recognized this fact and therefore concluded that the answer would be to apply the origin principle and equalize rates. However, the Committee also recognized that there would be a disturbance of revenue raising if this policy were adopted. It therefore concluded that the destination principle would have to be applied and fiscal frontiers would have to be tolerated.

It should be noted, however, that the destination principle may be acceptable if the goal is optimization of production, but it does not provide for the optimization of trade. This is so because the tax system influences the relative prices of X and Y in each country. Because of the excise duty in country I consumers there would buy more X and less Y than they would otherwise do, whilst in country II consumers would buy more Y and less X than would otherwise be the case. There would be a gain from a shift of X from country I to country II and a shift of Y from country II to country I.

If therefore we take account of what is required to optimize both production and trade, then neither the destination nor the origin principles are acceptable in themselves. What is indeed called for is a harmonization of duties and the adoption of the origin principle. This would then eliminate fiscal frontiers.

So much for the theoretical issues. In practice the Commission has been studying the problem in co-operation with national civil servants and has proposed as follows. In the case of manufactured tobacco, alcohol and alcoholic beverages, petroleum products and sugar, excise duties should be harmonized. Harmonization would take place in two stages – the first would deal with structures and the second with rates. The latter would provide for the abolition of tax frontiers. The adaptation of the excise systems of the various countries would fit in with the harmonization of turnover taxes. In the case of certain other products – beverages other than alcoholic and products which are substitutes for sugar – decisions can only be taken following more detailed examination of the problems involved. It is also proposed that excise duties can be abolished – that is, they can be built into the common TVA system – in the case of certain tropical products, salt, matches and playing cards. Certain local taxes and excise duties which do not affect intra-Community trade can be left unharmonized.

State Aids

Articles 92 and 94 of the Rome Treaty deal with state aids. Article 92 declares that, generally, state aids which distort or threaten to distort competition, by favouring certain enterprises or the production of certain goods, and which affect inter-state trade adversely, are incompatible with the Treaty. The Treaty does, however, state that some aids are acceptable. These are aids of a social character granted to individuals, e.g. free school milk, aids to make good damage caused by national disasters and aids to regions in West Germany which are disadvantaged by the division of Germany. In addition other forms of aid may be deemed compatible with the Treaty. These include assistance to promote the development of backward regions; to promote any important project of common European interest or to remedy a serious disturbance in an economy of a member state; to facilitate the development of certain activities or regions provided the aid does not affect trading conditions to such an extent as would be contrary to the common interest.

Virtually since the Treaty came into operation the Brussels Commission, as part of its day-to-day watchdog activity, has been attacking aids which it has deemed incompatible with the needs of integration. For example, in 1959 it turned its attention to a French fiscal aid. This concerned the practice by the French Government of granting more rapid depreciation for tax assessment in respect of purchases of French equipment. The Commission persuaded the French Government to modify the system. In 1960 the Commission persuaded the French to abandon aids for staple fibre production, silk spinning and *haute couture*. Governments are not, however, so imbued with Community spirit as to automatically comply with the requirements of the Commission.

One of the most prominent examples of state aids is to be found in the Community shipbuilding industry. This is particularly the case in France and Italy. In both countries direct subsidies have been given to enable the industry both to sell below its own cost of production and to convert to alternative lines of production. The Commission was originally hopeful that these aids could be progressively faded out. However, in attempting to secure this result the Commission encountered resistance from France and Italy. This resistance coincided with a deterioration in the competitive position of the Community in the world shipbuilding market. Whereas the Six accounted for 40 per cent of total world tonnage launched in 1954, by 1963 the figure was down to 28 per cent. As a result the Commission modified its position. It recognized that a common rate of subsidy of 10 per cent was justified on the grounds that this was the level of assistance enjoyed by Japanese producers. It proposed that this should be adopted by all the member-states for a trial period between 1967 and 1969.

State Monopolies and Public Purchasing

Within the Six a number of products are under the control of state trading monopolies. West Germany, France and Italy are the three states which have relied upon this system, the latter two in particular. For example, the supply of matches has been regulated by state monopolies in all three states and the supply of raw and manufactured tobacco in France and Italy. The basis of operation of these organizations is quite simple – by controlling supplies they can earn a monopoly income which is then paid to the state as part of its fiscal revenues. The Rome Treaty calls for member-states to adjust the mode of operation of these bodies so that by the end of the transition period no discrimination as regards supplies or markets exists between member-states. The Commission has sought to achieve such a result, but with limited success.

The policies adopted by member-states in respect of public purchasing also gives rise to very significant obstacles to the free and undistorted movement of goods. The size of public spending in modern western economies underlines the importance of this subject. The problem arises in connexion with the possibility that Government, both central and local as well as state-owned industries, do not proceed solely on the basis of commercial criteria but give a preference to domestic as opposed to foreign suppliers. From a European Parliamentary report (European Parliament, 22 March 1965), it appears that in virtually every EEC country the placing of building contracts takes place on a discriminatory basis. It is also interesting to note the observation of John Sheahan in his study of French industrial policy: 'The Government firms "buy French" with decidedly few exceptions' (Sheahan, 1963). It was alleged before the Select Committee on Nationalized Industries in 1962 that Electricité de France was firmly wedded to French suppliers. It was also alleged – though not proven – that Electricité de France allowed suppliers of equipment to recoup their research and development overheads in the prices charged for home orders, thus allowing exports to be sold below full cost (Select Committee on Nationalised Industries, 1963).

Technical and Administrative Obstacles

In all the member-states it is exceedingly common for Governments to lay down rules regarding the standards and qualities of goods sold on their national markets. This is a particularly desirable activity when consideration is given to the health and safety risks connected with the consumption and use of many goods. This activity does, however, pose a problem for those seeking to integrate national markets because these standards tend to differ, sometimes very markedly.

This type of Government influence is found, for example, in the case of motor vehicles in respect of such things as traffic indicators, braking and lighting systems and even windscreens. In connexion with the latter, since 1958 Italy has had a law which, on grounds of safety, stipulates that all cars must have laminated windscreens. On the other hand, some cars made in the Community, such as Volkswagen, have toughened windscreens made in a different way. Another example is provided by woollen garments. Under Belgian law pure wool means 97 per cent pure wool, whereas French law lays down a wool content of 85 per cent. In the field of food legislation, national standards are laid down in respect of colouring and preserving agents, and these differ widely from state to state. Pharmaceutical products, where a health risk clearly exists, are another field of government activity. Household electrical equipment and fittings exhibit considerable divergences – two-pin plugs vie with the three-pin variety and socket-fitting bulbs with the screw-fitting type. Such examples could be multiplied at length. The problem for integration is obvious. However efficient and competitive imported goods may be, they can be excluded if they do not meet the stipulated national standard. Differences do not always lead to this result. For example, the export of Volkswagens to Italy has not been prohibited. It has been suggested that this tolerance may be due to the fact that the German legislation prohibits cars whose doors open from front to rear and this is how Fiats used to be built. It is also true that even if national standards are enforced, trade need not be prevented. Producers could still export but it would be necessary to develop products to meet the technical requirements of each member-state.

This is highly undesirable. Much play has been made of the advantages which the US derives from the production of long runs of standardized goods for a huge home market. One of the obvious advantages of producing for a common market is the possibility of obtaining longer runs than those offered by relatively small national markets.

There is the further point that in, for example, the case of proprietary medicines, a product cannot normally be introduced on to a national market without the prior approval of the relevant national administrative body. The existence of such machinery gives rise to the possibility that foreign products could be deliberately kept off a national market since, where criteria are imprecise, or the reasons behind a decision are not made public, it would be difficult for foreign firms to prove a charge of discrimination.

This is therefore a field where vigorous harmonization of national legislative and administrative provisions, which is called for in Article 100 of the Rome Treaty, could pay great dividends. In practice the Brussels Commission has worked extremely hard on this subject and has produced a large number of draft regulations. Unfortunately few have been adopted. It is indeed doubtful whether the existing procedures are adequate to the task. Thus, in 1965 the Council of Ministers adopted a regulation relating to proprietary medicines. This concerned the unification of national procedures relating to requests to authorize the introduction of such products on national markets. An authorization under such a procedure is only valid in the state granting it. However, it should be noted that this first step does improve the position of a manufacturer in one state trying to obtain an authorization in another, since the conditions under which an authorization can be refused have been closely defined. This should reduce the possibility of outside producers being kept out for bogus reasons. It is, of course, obvious that the ultimate aim will have to be that an authorization granted in one state will be valid in all the others and a regulation to this effect has been drafted by the Commission, but as yet it has not been adopted by the Council of Ministers. The important point here is that the regulation relating to unification of procedures took two years to negotiate. First it had to be discussed by national experts, then it had to proceed through the

Economic and Social Council and the European Parliament, and it was only then that it could be finally thrashed out in the Council of Ministers. This is an exceptionally long-winded procedure, and it seems likely that it will take many years before the Community can work its way through all the products to which national standards are applied and in which significant differences as between states exist. Not only that, but there is a possibility that in the case of some products technical progress may be so rapid that European harmonized standards could lag behind such developments. The Commission appears to recognize this difficulty and has been proposing that where a Community standard is drawn up, and where the product is one in which technical progress is rapid and entails frequent alteration of technical norms, the Commission itself would be empowered to make the necessary changes. To assist it in this process an expert committee of representatives of member-states would be created. Only if this committee could not reach agreement would the matter of alterations be submitted to the Council of Ministers. It should, however, be emphasized that this procedure refers to the alteration of existing Community standards and that those standards in the first instance would have to be determined through Community procedures. Also, as already pointed out, this ability of the Commission to act on its own account would only apply in respect of particular products where technical progress is particularly rapid.

Cartels and Concentrations

Cartel and concentration policy in the Community plays a double role. At the time when the Rome Treaty was signed its main role was conceived as being one of assisting the process of integration. It was felt that some of the benefits of reducing tariff and quota barriers would be lost if there was no machinery for dealing with the activities of cartels and concentrated enterprises. This view was expressed by Commissioner Hans Von der Groeben, who, prior to the fusion of the Executives, was responsible for competition policy. In 1961, whilst speaking at the European Parliament, he put the matter thus:

it is . . . beyond dispute – and the authors of the Treaty were fully aware of this – that it would be useless to bring down trade barriers between

Member States if the Governments or private industry were to remain free through economic and fiscal legislation, through subsidies or cartel-like restrictions on competition, virtually to undo the opening of the markets and to prevent, or at least unduly to delay, the action needed to adapt them to the Common Market (European Parliamentary Assembly Debate, 1961).

However, more recently a second role has come to the fore. It is now recognized that concentration policy must not merely be concerned with controlling concentrations in the interests of maintaining competition, but also with facilitating them. The word 'facilitating' requires interpretation. In France it would certainly mean actively encouraging the process of concentration. The Brussels Commission, on the other hand, takes the view that any factors which artificially discourage concentration should be swept away. It would equally argue that any factors which artificially encourage concentration should likewise be eliminated. The argument advanced in favour of 'facilitating' concentration is two-fold. Firstly, the emergence of an enlarged Community market enables concentration to take place without creating the market power problems which would arise in smaller national markets. Secondly, a policy of facilitating concentration is required in order that Community industry shall be able to compete with the giant enterprises of the US. Such a policy is concerned with equalizing the conditions of Atlantic competition. It is maintained that the greater size of US enterprises confers upon them the advantage of the economies of large-scale production and also enables them to mount the research and development programmes which are beyond the means of the majority of Community firms. On the cartel side, too, the Brussels Commission recognizes that greater efficiency and greater scales of output can be achieved by the approval of joint purchasing arrangements, and by relaxing the rules relating to common research, rationalization and specialization agreements. This concern with increasing the scale of enterprises and obtaining greater efficiency can be said to be called for by Article 2 of the Rome Treaty which states that one of the aims of the Community shall be the achievement of an accelerated raising of the standard of living in the Six.

However, this second aspect of Community cartel and concentration policy will be reserved for discussion in chapter 7. Here we shall be concerned with cartels and concentrations as possible inhibitors of intra-Community trade and competition across frontiers.

There are two ways of indicating how cartels and concentrations inhibit integration. We can *a priori* imagine all the ways in which cartels and concentrations might operate to this end. Alternatively, we can adopt an empirical approach and consider actual examples. We will follow the latter course.

During the course of the investigations of the UK Monopolies Commission, the French Commission Technique Des Ententes, and above all the Brussels Commission, a wide variety of international cartel practices affecting trade between the Six have been brought to light. They indicate that, despite the buoyant state of international trade in the post-war years and the persistence of full employment and economic growth, international cartels are still much in evidence.

A form of practice which is quite common in the Community is the common sales agency or syndicate. It seems quite usual within the Six for national producers to carry out their export, and for that matter, home sales business by means of common selling syndicates. Practice varies but typically the members of the syndicate, although basically independent, assign their output to the syndicate organization which then arranges sales and fixes a common selling price. Thus in the case of the Comptoir Française de l'Azote (CFA), twenty-eight French nitrogenous fertilizer producers entrusted to it the sale of all or part of their production both at home and abroad (including the EEC). The CFA is a limited company and the firms holding shares in it delivered their produce to it and the Comptoir fixed a common selling price for sales in France and paid the uniform price to all producers at the end of the year. Exports were sold at a price fixed by the CFA after discussion with dealers, and producers were paid the home price for export sales. The deficit arising from the lower price in the export market was financed by contributions from all producers proportional to their output and irrespective of whether or not they exported. Belgium nitrogenous fertilizer producers channelled their home and export sales through a common selling syndicate, the Comptoir Belge de L'Azote (Cobelaz). French producers of gypsum have utilized a similar sales method – quotas were allocated both for home and export sales and the syndicate fixed a common selling price.

These are examples of arrangements between national groups to eliminate competition between themselves in the export field. In addition, cases have come to light of cartel agreements which are truly international in character in that firms from several states of the Community participate. The Monopolies Commission threw light on two examples, the Lausanne Arrangement and the Lausanne Agreement. The former related to cable and the latter to copper and copper-based alloys. In both cases firms from several EEC states took part and the basis of the agreements was that firms, when selling into a national market, would align their offers on the price levels of domestic producers. Then again in 1961 the Commission Technique Des Ententes reported the existence of an international cartel agreement between linoleum producers. One of the rules of the cartel was that members selling linoleum in France should align their quotations on the price offered by the French members.

Market sharing is quite a common practice. This takes two forms. One is sharing by agreement. The other arises when national groups decide independently to keep out of each other's way. In 1961 the German Federal Cartel Office brought to light an agreement whereby trade in adhesive tape between West Germany and the Netherlands was restricted. In 1954 a gentleman's agreement was concluded which required that German producers should no longer supply the Dutch market (with the exception of one large buyer) and the Dutch for their part should keep out of the West German market. In 1962 the Commission Technique Des Ententes reported that French producers of certain agricultural implements were party to an international cartel agreement which assigned them a virtual monopoly of the French market on the understanding that they kept out of the national markets of other members. The Brussels Commission has also dealt with a market-sharing agreement between Dutch and Belgian enterprises producing detergents.

There is some evidence of oligopolistic behaviour as between national groups. Prior to the bringing to light of the activities of the CFA and Cobelaz, it was noted that Community fertilizer producers had large export trades to third countries but there was comparatively little inter-trading within the Six. This was particularly surprising in view of the fact that prices in third country markets were low as compared with prices within the Community. When the Brussels Commission reported on the activities of the CFA it provided support for the oligopolistic hypothesis since what emerged was that it was the deliberate policy of the CFA to avoid competing with producers in other member-states. Further evidence of this type of behaviour was provided by the Brussels Commission in 1968 when it reported on the activities of producers of semi-finished metal products. The Commission noted that

according to the manufacturers concerned, the main reasons for their agreement had been a fear that manufacturers of these products in the four other countries involved, who had not made any corresponding agreement, would react to entry into their home markets by trying themselves to sell on the home markets of the parties to the agreement (EEC Commission, 1967, p. 65).

Quota fixing is another way in which inter-state trade and competition is restricted. One of the most important examples of this was the Noordwijk Cement Agreement concluded in 1956 between twenty-eight Belgian, two Dutch and six German cement-producting firms. Dutch producers were unable to meet national demands in their market and therefore outside producers were allowed to sell in the Dutch market, but the competition thus created was regulated by the agreement. The parties agreed quotas for deliveries of cement clinker to the Dutch market, and collectively fixed prices. They also undertook not to erect plant in each other's countries without obtaining the consent of the relevant parties.

Exclusive dealing is an obvious way of restricting inter-state trade. A group of producers can bind dealers to buy exclusively from them. The more that dealers within a national market enter into such exclusive arrangements, the more difficult it is for firms outside the producing group to penetrate that market. The

Commission has uncovered such cases in respect of Belgian, Dutch and West German producers of wall and floor tiles selling in the Belgian market, Belgian, Dutch and German producers of sand and gravel selling in the Belgian and Dutch markets and producers of water heaters selling in Belgium and Luxembourg.

One way in which national cartels can exclude imports from the home market is by the system of aggregated rebates. Several cases have come to light in West Germany of syndicates granting individual buyers rebates, the size of which increased in line with the size of their total annual purchases from the group as a whole. On the one hand it has to be recognized that a greater volume of purchases may lead to greater economies in production and thus justify, at least in some degree, such a progressive rebate scale. But, on the other hand, it is clear that foreign firms can be put at a disadvantage. A purchaser who decides to import may as a result enjoy a lower level of rebate (than otherwise) on the whole of his purchases from the national producing group, and a foreign supplier will therefore have to put in a commensurately low bid to compensate the purchaser.

When we come to the question of concentrated enterprises and how they can inhibit inter-state trade, we find the Community case-book barren and we therefore have to rely on hypothetical examples. It is not difficult, however, to envisage how such enterprises might undo the work of trade liberalization, particularly if we consider national experience both in the Six and outside. One example is based on the role which transport costs could play. Thus a firm which enjoyed a dominant position in the Italian market could operate a price discrimination policy as between the North and the South. In the North, where competition from enterprises in the EEC states was a possibility, it could charge artificially low prices in order to keep competitors out. In the South, where transport costs would limit the competition from outside supplies, it could charge a relatively high price and recoup any losses made on northern sales. The activities of German cement-producing firms suggest that this is a real possibility. Alternatively, a firm which is dominant in a national market could buttress its position by entering into exclusive dealing agreements with the main dealers in that market. Foreign firms would then encounter difficulties in penetrating that market because of a lack of outlets.

The Rome Treaty recognizes the existence of this type of problem, and Articles 85 and 86 of the Treaty specifically deal with it. Briefly, Article 85 (1) prohibits a wide range of collusive practices, and Article 85 (2) declares them null and void – that is, unenforceable in the courts. However, Article 85 (3) establishes a 'gateway' by means of which otherwise prohibited practices can be legalized.

Article 85 cites examples of prohibited practices such as agreements by competitors to abide by a common price. The agreement in question must, however, be designed to, or actually result in, the prevention, restriction or distortion of competition *within* the Common Market. It must also – and this is of the highest importance in the light of the subject matter of this chapter – be likely to affect trade between member-states. For an agreement to be exempted it must improve the production and distribution of goods or promote technical and economic progress. It is also necessary that the customer should enjoy a fair share of the resulting profit or benefit, and the agreement must not involve any restriction which is not indispensable to the achievement of these objectives. In addition, the agreement must not enable the enterprises concerned to *eliminate* competition in respect of a *substantial* part of the goods involved.

Article 86 refers not to concentrations but to firms which are in a dominant position. Moreover, the dominant position in question is one in the Common Market or a substantial part thereof. A dominant position itself is not prohibited; what is prohibited is an abuse thereof, which takes the form of, for example, the imposition of unfair selling or buying prices and the limitation of production.

What, then, have these Articles achieved? As far as Article 86 is concerned the Community casebook, as we have already said, appears to be barren and we shall therefore confine the discussion to activities under Article 85. The Commission is the effective watchdog in this field of policy and to assist it in locating offending agreements three forms of machinery are employed. In the first place the Commission has established a system of notification.

Apart from the fact that this enables the Commission to be informed of restrictive practices which require scrutiny, the mechanism also enables firms to establish the legality or otherwise of their practices. Even if a practice is eventually found inadmissible, parties to it are protected from fines during the period from timely notification until a decision is reached by the Commission.

Under the notification scheme parties to an agreement can apply for what is known as a negative clearance. That is to say, a declaration from the Commission that it has no grounds to interfere with the practice in question. However, the practice may be one which does offend against Article 85. In such a case several possibilities are opened up. One is that parties may be able to prove benefits which enable the agreement to be exempted under Article 85 (3). They may not, however, be able to secure such exemptions without modification of the agreement. Then again the agreement may not be exempted even with modification in which case the parties to it can voluntarily terminate the agreement, or the Commission can make a formal decision to the effect that the agreement is prohibited. To continue thereafter to practise the agreement would leave the parties open to fines.

Apart from notification, the Commission is able to obtain information about potentially harmful practices by its system of complaints. This has been of considerable importance. The Commission can also initiate an investigation where the trend of inter-state trade suggests the existence of an agreement. This technique has been utilized in respect of trade in margarine.

Turning now to cases, a good deal of the early activity of the Commission was concerned with a practice which has not yet been referred to, namely bilateral exclusive dealing. When firms export, it is quite common for them to appoint an independent firm as the exclusive dealer of its products in a particular territory. Thus a German firm, when selling to France, may appoint a particular firm as the sole dealer of its goods in France. More important still, it has been the practice to confer upon the dealer absolute territorial protection. Thus, to continue our example, sole dealers in the Netherlands, Belgium and so forth would be banned from supplying the good in question to the French market. As a result of this compartmentalization of the Common Market, different prices for the same product can exist in the various national markets. In the absence of territorial protection (and differences in indirect taxes) price variations would tend to be ironed out by the movement of goods from low-priced to high-priced markets.

Since the Commission seeks to create a common market in which conditions resemble those of the national market, it is not surprising that it should attack a practice which had led to marked price differentials. This issue came to a head in the now celebrated Grundig-Consten case, the basic facts of which are as follows. Grundig appointed Consten of Paris sole dealer of certain forms of radio and electronic equipment in France, and in addition – and this was to prove of the highest importance – conferred on Consten absolute territorial protection by banning Grundig dealers in all the other countries of the Six from supplying the French market. It transpired, however, that Consten's rival firm in Paris, UNEF, obtained Grundig products from wholesalers in Germany and sold them at more favourable prices. Consten approached the French Court of Appeal but the latter refused to deliver a judgement pending a decision by the Brussels Commission. As a result of this the Commission found that its hand was forced.

The Commission was able to show that there were considerable differences in prices of the agreement-goods as between Germany and France. In 1962 the actual catalogue price (less discounts) of a particular Grundig recorder was 23 per cent higher in France than Germany (after deduction of customs duties and taxes the difference was 44 per cent). The Commission pointed out that the arrangement restricted competition, and that the sole distributorship, plus territorial protection, effectively put Consten in a monopoly position at its stage of the distributive process. An effect on inter-state trade was obvious – other importers were banned from importing Grundig products. The Commission had to consider whether exemption under Article 85 (3) could be accorded, but decided against taking such a step. It was prepared to accept that sole dealing improved production and distribution and it therefore concentrated its attack on two other points. As we have seen Article 85 requires that an agreement should allow a fair share of the profits to accrue to consumers – but the higher prices in France clearly indicated that this did not occur. That Article also requires that the restrictions in an agreement should be no more than necessary to achieve the improvements in production and distribution. The Commission was able to show that many improvements did not require sole dealing backed up by territorial protection. For example, Grundig argued that unofficial importers would not carry out guarantee and after-sales service and this would damage its reputation. Moreover, they would leave these tasks to Consten. The Commission countered by saying that these services were the responsibility of the supplier and could not be off-loaded – in any case suppliers would be forced by competition to provide such services. Moreover, if Consten was approached to provide after-sales service for goods it had not sold, this could still be financially worth-while.

The decision was appealed to the European Court of Justice. Briefly, the upshot appears to have been that although the Court did not uphold the Commission's ban on the agreement in its entirety, it certainly upheld it in so far as territorial protection gave Consten a monopoly of Grundig products at its stage in the distribution chain and created a price differential between the German and the French markets. The position taken by the Court of Justice has enabled the Commission to launch an attack on practices which compartmentalize the Common Market. Thus in 1968 the Commission, acting on the basis of a complaint, discovered that it was a widespread practice among West German toy manufacturers to grant exclusive selling rights in memberstates and to reinforce this by imposing export bans. The Commission declared that the export bans were contrary to the Rome Treaty, and they have been lifted.

The Commission has also taken up a position in respect of simple exclusive dealing – that is, where there is no territorial protection. It has maintained that a restriction affecting interstate trade exists where, for example, the agreement is a reciprocal one and the parties voluntarily restrict their trade relationship to each other, and outside dealers in one state cannot get supplies from the producer but must resort to dealers in other memberstates. However, the Commission has granted exemption under

Article 85 (3) in that such agreements help to improve distribution. Exports can be concentrated on one dealer rather than through a multiplicity of outlets, and this concentration enables a better overall view to be obtained of the development of a particular national market. The Commission has in fact decided that, following the conferment upon it of the power to exempt whole categories of agreements, it will apply this in respect of simple exclusive dealing agreements provided they are not encumbered by clauses which provide territorial protection.

Although distribution agreements can clearly inhibit the creation of a truly common market, it is obvious that the horizontal cartel agreements of the price-fixing, market-sharing variety must be high on the list of practices which the Commission needs to investigate. In the case of the French nitrogen fertilizer syndicate (CFA), the Commission refused to grant an application for a negative clearance for the agreement as it stood, and as a result the syndicate had to abandon a number of objectionable practices. In particular the syndicate will not be allowed to intervene in export sales to other member-states; these will have to be negotiated on an individual basis. However, in respect of other sales – internal and in non-member countries – the syndicate can continue to operate as before. It is, however, open to question whether, given the opportunity for such collaboration, the firms will act independently in respect of intra-Community trade. The Commission has also dealt with the Belgian syndicate (Cobelaz) in much the same way. It has also stipulated that no restriction is to be placed on Belgian wholesalers and dealers respecting the importing and exporting of fertilizers. In short, if there are differences in prices as between member-states, dealers are not to be restrained from moving supplies and evening prices out. This may help to break down the oligopolistic stalemate. In the case of the French gypsum syndicate the requirements of the Commission were so rigorous that the firms which were party to it decided to terminate the arrangement.

In the case of market sharing, the Commission has attacked a number of agreements. The market-sharing agreement between Dutch and Belgian manufacturers of detergents, and the agreement relating to semi-finished metal products referred to earlier, have both been prohibited and as a result the parties to them have dissolved them. The Commission also encountered another market-sharing agreement among producers of building materials. All the members, except one, of an association in member-state A agreed not to export to member-state B. The exempted firm agreed not to export to member-state B more than a specified absolute amount per annum. This firm also obtained the agreement of nearly all the producers in member-state B to the effect that they would not export to member-state A. The agreement was defended on the grounds of the threat of economic disturbance. The Commission did not accept this defence. It prohibited the agreement which was subsequently dissolved.

In the case of quotas the Commission prohibited the agreement relating to the sale of silica in the Dutch market by Dutch, Belgian and German firms. Exclusive-dealing agreements referred to earlier in connexion with sand and gravel, and water heaters, together with one more recently relating to the import of timber into Belgium, have also been terminated following action by the Brussels Commission.

More recently the Commission has increasingly begun to show its teeth in dealing with cartel practices. Early in 1969 it banned an agreement between a group of German, French and Belgian semi-finished metal makers which involved the fixing of uniform prices and conditions of sale in the Dutch market. The Italian nitrate fertilizer sales cartel SEIFA was also attacked and as a result, in respect of sales to the rest of the Community, producers and dealers are required to deal direct rather than through the cartel. The Commission also turned its attention to the activities of the International Cable Development Corporation. Arrangements were devised to provide reciprocal protection of national markets. These included bans on investment or the acquisition of shares together with a refusal to supply purchasers in countries belonging to the organization or to sell except on the same terms as companies established there. But the two most significant cases are those in which the Commission exercised its power to fine. In 1969 six firms, who controlled 80 per cent of the Community quinine market and had been found to be engaged in price fixing and market sharing were fined a total of $500,000. About the same time ten companies (one was ICI), referred to as the 'Analine Trust', were fined $485,000 for operating concerted practices. They were accused of engineering similar and more or less simultaneous prices increases in analine dyes in 1964 and 1965 and attempting to do so again in 1967.

This account is, of course, far from exhaustive; it is merely illustrative of the Commission's activities in this field. It should also be pointed out that a study merely confined to the more formal decisions would give a very inadequate picture of the Commission's activity. In many cases firms are inclined to terminate their agreements when challenged by the Commission and the matters are therefore dealt with before the stage of formal proceedings is reached. A considerable amount of activity of this kind is continually taking place though unfortunately the Commission releases little information about it. Although the Commission was slow to get off the mark, and many of its early decisions were concerned with bilateral distribution agreements, there is now a growing body of evidence to the effect that the Commission is becoming increasingly vigorous in the field of traditional horizontal cartel agreements. There does, however, remain a remarkable lack of activity in the field of firms occupying a dominant position.

4 Factor Movements

The Free Movement of Labour

In keeping with the concept of a common market, as opposed to a customs union, the Rome Treaty provides for the free movement of labour. (There is a provision that freedom of movement can be limited on grounds of public safety, public security and public health.) Article 48 requires that free movement be achieved before the end of the transition period. In fact in this sphere of operations the EEC has registered a distinct success in that complete freedom of movement was achieved in July 1968, one and a half years ahead of schedule. It should be noted that free movement does not apply to employment in public administration. It has, however, been pointed out that this provision

is nothing like as restrictive as it sounds. No official regulations or codes of practice have been adopted and the position varies somewhat from one member country to another, but in actual fact virtually nobody is prevented from moving to another country even if he is a public employee. The onus is on the receiving country, which is usually happy to employ foreign manual workers in nationalised industries or local government. Professional and technical people are unlikely to be employed in a public service or nationalised industry of another country and no foreigner in any category is likely to be employed in national Government service (Beever, 1969).

Article 48 complements the principle of free movement with a ban on discrimination based on nationality in regard to employment, remuneration and other conditions of work.

The Community approached the establishment of free movement of labour in stages. The first, which was provided for in Council Regulation 15 of 1961, operated between September 1961 and May 1964. During this period the movement of labour into another member-state required the issue of a permit by the state of destination. Workers were permitted to renew the permit for the same occupation after one year of regular employment. After three years they were able to renew their permit for any other occupation for which they were qualified and after four years for any kind of paid work. In effect after four years discrimination ceased. During this first period a preference was given to national workers in that any vacancies in the national labour market were compulsorily notified for three weeks in the labour exchanges of the home country but after this period offers of employment were transmitted to other member-states. But if, for example, an employer asked for a worker by name the temporary preference for home market supply could be waived. During this stage also a Community preference existed in that Community workers were to have priority over workers from third countries in filling job vacancies.

During the second stage, which extended from May 1964 to June 1968, progressive freedom under the permit system was speeded up in that after two years of regular employment a migrant worker could move to any job on the same terms as nationals. The national preference was abolished but a safeguard clause was inserted which enabled a member-state to restore it for fifteen days when a surplus of manpower existed in certain areas or trades. If a member-state operated the safeguard clause it had to be justified adequately. Apparently

the states have used this right infrequently. Germany, Italy and Luxemburg did not use it at all. The Netherlands and Belgium made use of it three months during 1965 for show artists and musicians. France made use of this right for office workers and distributive trade employees. Finally both Belgium and France re-introduced the clause for some of their regions (Yannopoulos, 1969).

The priority of Community workers over non-Community workers was preserved.

In July 1968 complete freedom of movement became a reality. The principle of national priority was abandoned and so Community workers can now have the same access to jobs as nationals. Work permits have been abolished and as a result Common Market migrant workers can take up employment without having to comply with any formalities other than those for residence permits. The latter are issued for a period of five years and are renewable automatically. The priority of Community workers over non-Community workers has, however, been retained.

It hardly needs saying that complete freedom of movement could not have become a reality unless a lot of other problems had been dealt with. To take two examples, workers need to be informed of job opportunities in other member-states and social security rights need to be transferable. In order to deal with the problem of job information the Community has established a European Co-ordinating Office (European Office for the Co-ordination and Balancing of Employment Supply and Demand). A system has been established whereby the member-states inform each other about supplies of surplus manpower and offers of employment. The actual process of clearing is, however, very much a decentralized business carried out by the employment exchanges of the member-states. The Commission has assisted by introducing advanced courses for government specialists in vacancy clearing activities. It has also helped to improve the clearing system by introducing a standardized terminology in respect of the description of occupations. The office produces quarterly surveys of the situation in and development of the labour markets in the member-states. An annual report on vacancy clearing operations is also produced as well as a forecast for the coming year.

A generous level of social security benefits would be a considerable deterrent to labour mobility if a migrant worker had to sacrifice them on moving to another member-state. At a relatively early date therefore the Community addressed itself to the problem of the social security of migrant workers. The main principles of the treatment of migrant workers are these. Firstly, a migrant worker is accorded similar treatment to a national. Thus if an Italian worker takes his family to Belgium, he receives family allowances at the Belgian level. Secondly, in determining the right to benefits and the calculation of them all insurance periods valid in the law of the various member-states shall be added together.

It was also necessary to deal with other matters where migrant workers were discriminated against. For example, in the 1961 Regulation foreign workers were made eligible to vote for candidates to works councils in host firms. The Commission sought to render them eligible to be candidates but this did not prove acceptable. When a foreign worker moved from one state to another the 1961 Regulation allowed him to take his wife and minor children only and also required that he should have acquired 'normal' housing for his family. In the 1964 Regulation the Commission made some progress. A worker became eligible for election to a workers' council provided he had worked for three years with the firm and fulfilled the same conditions for eligibility as national workers. Not only that but the definition of family was expanded to cover not only the wife and minor children, but all children, parents and grandparents dependent on the worker. Although some of these issues seem to be relatively innocuous they were in fact the subject of keen bargaining and debate between the member-states (see Dahlberg, 1968).

Migrant workers have of course got to face the problems of adjusting to a new environment and obtaining housing accommodation. In 1962 the Commission sent a recommendation to member-states to the effect that they should promote services to assist migrants on arrival in host countries. In 1965 in another recommendation the Commission drew attention to the need for improvements in the provision of housing. As will be seen later, in 1965 the Commission suggested that the tasks of the European Social Fund should be redefined so as to include assistance in connexion with the provision of such accommodation.

Some studies have been undertaken of the trend and pattern of migration within the Community. One study (Yannopoulos, 1969), based on the years 1958 to 1965 inclusive, reveals the following facts. The number of work permits granted for the first time to foreign workers (intra-Community migration) rose from 156,000 in 1958 to 305,000 in 1965. In 1958 and 1959 the main recipient was France with Germany second. However, since 1960 Germany has been far and away the largest recipient. In 1965 80 per cent of all permits issued in respect of intra-Community migration were for movements to West Germany. Italy is the main provider of migrant labour – between 1958 and 1965 the Italian percentage of total Community workers migrating ranged from 75 per cent to 83 per cent. There was also good evidence that migratory flows were related to relative wage levels. Countries with the relatively highest wage costs per hour (manual workers) participated most in intra-Community immigration and vice-versa. It is also interesting to note that as the differentials in hourly earnings progressively narrowed over the period, intra-Community migration became proportionately less important and the supply of labour from non-member countries became proportionately more important.

The Free Movement of Capital

There are three main strands in Community policy in respect of the capital market. Firstly, as in the case of labour, the Rome Treaty calls for mobility of capital as between member-state economies. Hindering factors must be swept away. Secondly, it is desirable and indeed necessary that all factors which distort the allocation of capital as between member-states should be eliminated. Thirdly, there is a need to deal with some of the inadequacies of existing capital markets in order to render them more in tune with the present needs of the economies of the Six.

The Treaty rules

The Rome Treaty provision in respect of the capital market are found in Articles 67 to 73. The basic provision is to be found in Article 67. It states that during the transition period, and to the extent necessary to ensure the proper functioning of the Common Market, member-states will abolish all restrictions on the movement of capital belonging to persons resident in the Six. Also discrimination based on nationality, on the place of residence of such persons or on the place where the capital is to be invested shall be abolished. Article 67 also requires that current payments connected with the movement of capital should be freed of all restrictions by the end of the first stage of the transition period.

According to Article 68 national rules governing the capital and money markets must, when applied to freed capital movements, be exercised in a non-discriminatory manner. Article 71 contains a standstill requirement. Member-states shall endeavour to avoid introducing within the Six any new exchange restrictions on the movement of capital and current payments connected therewith, and shall endeavour not to render existing regulations more restrictive. Article 73 contains a safeguard clause. If the movement of capital disturbs the capital market of a member-state, the Commission shall, after the Monetary Committee has been consulted, authorize such a state to take protective measures in the field of capital movements. The Council may, however, revoke such a decision. A member-state may, however, on grounds of secrecy or urgency, take measures without prior approval. In such a case the Commission and other member-states must be informed of the measures not later than the date when they come into effect. However, the Commission, after consulting the Monetary Committee, may amend or abolish such measures. Whilst dealing with emergency measures we should also take note of Article 109 which relates to balance-of-payments policy. Briefly, that Article allows a member-state in case of a sudden crisis to take necessary protective measures, which could include control of capital movements.

Inhibitions

With the formal rules behind us, the subject which now falls due for consideration is the degree to which the Community has dealt with those factors which hinder the free movement of capital. The basic position is that the Community has introduced some liberalizing measures but a completely free capital market cannot as yet be said to exist. In some degree this reluctance to free capital completely may be ascribed to a fear on the part of member-states that the life-blood, capital, will ebb away if all controls are relinquished. However, in 1960 and 1962 directives were introduced which provided a significant degree of loosening up. The provisions in these directives can be divided into two categories. Unconditional freedom of movement was accorded in the case of direct investment, operations in listed securities, personal capital movements, investment in real estate and short- and medium-term credits linked with commercial transactions and the rendering of services. Unconditional in this sense refers to the fact that freedom can only be revoked under the emergency provisions of Articles 73 and 109. Conditional liberalization was established for the issue of unlisted securities on capital markets and medium- and long-term financial loans and credits (i.e. those not connected with commercial transactions). Conditional in this sense refers to the fact that member-states can apply restrictions to these types of transactions if the movements of capital involved are such as to impede the achievement of the objectives of a member-state's economic policies. Three member-states – France, Italy and the Netherlands – have taken advantage of this clause to maintain partial or total restrictions.

Apart from the fact that capital movements are far from entirely free of Government control, the Segré Report of 1966 (*The Development of a European Capital Market*) also referred to the inhibiting effects observed in the field of exchange rates. There are two such effects. Firstly, in some cases there has been a free exchange rate for capital transactions as opposed to an official exchange rate for current operations and the fluctuations in the capital market have been greater than those in the current market. The possibility of a loss has therefore been an inhibiting factor. Secondly, in the view of the Segré Report even the official fluctuations are undesirable and it is argued that in the long term these too should be eliminated.

Distortions

The Segré Report also drew attention to a number of factors which distort the working of the Community capital market. One is the international double taxation of income from securities. Thus the payment of a dividend to an individual resident in a country different from that in which the Company is incorporated may attract double taxation. A withholding tax would be applied in the country of incorporation. A tax would also be applied in the country of the shareholder's domicile. Clearly the lack of double taxation conventions is bound to deter the movement of capital between those countries which have not entered into such arrangements. Another factor is the practice of discriminating in terms of taxation in favour of income from shares in companies incorporated at home as opposed to income from shares in companies incorporated abroad. Clearly this inhibits investment in other member-states. A third source of distortion arises out of the practice of non-resident shareholders collecting their income in the country of incorporation. In some cases the withholding tax levied in the country of incorporation is at a fixed rate which is lower than the marginal rate which would apply in the country of the shareholders' domicile. Under these circumstances where, as is sometimes the case, the tax authorities in the state of domicile are uninformed of the income in question, it pays shareholders to collect their dividends in the source country. It is fairly obvious that such arrangements may be a way of attracting cheap capital to the source country.

Any discussion of the distorting effects on the distribution of the Community's capital resources would be incomplete without reference to differences as between member-states in the rate of taxation on income from investment. Although the Rome Treaty makes no explicit reference to the need for harmonization of direct taxation, Articles 100 to 102 dealing with the approximation of laws provide the basis for a solution where discrepancies interfere with competition and produce distortions. Theoretically speaking, discrepancies in the rate of tax can give rise to problems. Suppose that member-state A levies a tax of 50 per cent whilst member-state B is content with 25 per cent. Other things being equal capital will flow from A to B until the accumulation of capital in B leads to an equalization in the rates of return net of tax in both countries. But if the rates of return net of tax are equal then it follows that the returns *before tax* must be unequal. This in turn implies that the distribution of the productive factor capital is distorted. (We are of course assuming that businessmen seek to maximize returns net of tax.) Economic reasoning therefore suggests that distortions could arise but whether a problem really exists depends on the facts. An empirical investigation, published in 1965, suggests that there is indeed a problem. For example, in the case of a West German corporation investing in a corporation in another member-state, the tax on income from investment would be between 27 per cent and 7 per cent lower than if investment was made in West Germany. This example relates to an investment in a subsidiary (substantial interest), earnings being fully retained (Musgrave, 1965).

The problem was considered by the Fiscal and Financial Committee chaired by Professor Fritz Neumark. It suggested that the member-states should equalize their profits taxes – 50 per cent on ploughed back profits and 25 per cent and not less than 15 per cent, on distributions being the suggested rates. It should, however, be noted that the Community has not yet taken any step to harmonize direct taxes. The position of the Neumark Committee is, of course, in marked contrast to past British experience which has tended to discriminate against distributed profits. The Neumark proposal should be regarded as an important contribution towards the achievement of a rational allocation of capital as between alternative uses.

We shall in connexion with the later discussion of social security harmonization consider the possibility that social security costs of production can be passed on by entrepreneurs to labour. Equally, the possibility exists that taxes on income from investment could be shifted on to the consumer in the form of higher prices. It should be noted, however, that under conditions of international perfect competition the tax cannot be shifted. An equalization of tax rates would therefore equalize burdens on entrepreneurs and prevent distortions. The removal of trade barriers and the action of the Anti-trust Division of the Commission are of course measures which create a market situation in which shifting becomes more difficult.

Tax harmonization

This discussion of the equalization of taxes on income from investment provides an opportunity to discuss the general implications of harmonization. To the extent that harmonization is achieved the freedom of action of member-state Governments will be circumscribed. We have seen that an equalization of the rates of turnover tax and excise duties is probable. If direct taxes were also harmonized then a member-state Government would find that, with a given national income, and a given distribution thereof, the revenue it could raise would be determined for it. But a Government might wish to raise more (or less) revenue than the amount it was forced to raise. This argument suggests that complete tax harmonization is likely to meet with some opposition from member-state governments and progress may therefore be slow. Indeed, slow progress is highly likely since, as has already been pointed out, the Rome Treaty is only specific on the subject of harmonization of indirect taxes.

It is only fair to point out that the Neumark Committee did not envisage a harmonization of taxes on income from employment, the reason behind this being that labour is generally less mobile than capital and therefore the possibility of distorting movements is less likely. Nevertheless the harmonization of taxation (other than that on income from employment) could limit a member-state's ability to raise revenue. For example, Italy's desire to deal with the South could be impeded. One way of dealing with such a problem would be to arrange for an international redistribution of tax revenues. Needless to say, this would be a controversial issue although, as we shall see in later discussions of Community financial arrangements, significant international redistributions of income have occurred.

Modernizing the capital market

The Segré Report in discussing the European capital market has drawn attention to a number of its weaknesses and has called for structural developments. Space does not permit a discussion of all its present limitations but two in particular are worth noting. The first relates to the lack of an adequately developed supply of long-term risk capital. The saving potential of the EEC has not been deficient; for example, between 1960 and 1964 savings rose at an annual average rate of 9·5 per cent and thus far out-stripped the growth of the Gross National Product. Unfortunately, the saving public prefers safe and liquid assets. As a result, as compared with the UK and US, a far greater proportion of savings are channelled via savings banks, commercial banks and the Post Office. These institutions tend to invest the public's savings in fixed interest securities. In fact what is needed is the development of insurance companies and the like which are prepared to channel contractual savings into industrial ordinary shares. This is all the more important as many firms are already heavily burdened with interest charges and cannot absorb more capital of a fixed-interest kind.

Another factor which deters investment in ordinary shares is the limited size of the domestic stock market. Because of this, sales of sizeable blocks of shares tend to glut the market and drive the price down against the seller. The reverse arises in the case of purchases. Price movements therefore occur which would be regarded as abnormal in London or New York.

The Freedom to Supply Services and the Right of Establishment

The Rome Treaty also provides that during the transition period restrictions which limit the ability of nationals of one member-state to set up in business in another member-state shall be removed. Also that just as individuals and companies under the Treaty enjoy increasing freedom in supplying goods to individuals and companies in other member-states, so they shall be progressively freer to supply services. Slow progress has been made in these fields largely because three problems obtrude. One is that there is little point in being nominally free to supply a service in another member-state if the professional qualification obtained in one member-state is not recognized in another. A great deal of work is therefore needed in the sphere of national recognition of diplomas and of co-ordination of conditions for admission to and practise in the liberal professions. By its very nature progression in this field is extremely time consuming. The second problem relates to the practice of partly or wholly preventing firms in other member-states from tendering for work for central or local Governments and other bodies which conclude contracts under public law. The third problem relates to the difficulties which arise for companies as a result of differences in the company laws of the various member-states. For example, laws differ in respect of protection of shareholders against companies and the protection of companies against debtors. The Commission has been active in both these latter fields.

5 Common Policies

It is undoubtedly true that much of the Community policy is based on a free market and competition. The removal of tariff and non-tariff barriers, and the introduction of an anti-trust policy relating to inter-state trade, all provide evidence for this view. The important role played by competition has not been denied by the staff of the EEC Commission. One senior member put it thus: 'It is . . . no exaggeration to state that economically, the Rome Treaty is basically a Treaty for more competition . . . [competition] has been considered as one of the principal pillars on which our building rests' (Mussard, 1962). Nevertheless, not all Community policy is based on the free-market concept. The common policies for agriculture, transport and energy all presuppose the existence of markets which are in some degree managed. This is most obviously so in the case of agriculture where price levels are not left to the free play of market forces. Quite the contrary, in some cases the market will be manipulated so as to bring about predetermined price levels. These will be managed with a number of ends in view, one of which will be the guarantee of an adequate income for the farming population. Then again the common agricultural policy is deeply involved in changing the farm structure and, as we shall see later, this will be a major element of policy in the 1970s. In the case of transport a management element is also apparent and, as in agriculture, the common policy bears a considerable resemblance to the national regimes which preceeded it. Community transport policy is, however, something of a compromise between the more rigidly controlled systems, such as that of West Germany, and the freer philosophy of the Netherlands. Under this policy certain transport rates are not to be free but are to be constrained within administratively determined rate brackets. Then again the blueprints of the common policy do appear to contemplate the continuance of licensing. In the case of energy the management element is the least obvious since as yet little has been achieved. At present the policy is more a statement of what needs to be done rather than of what has been accomplished. Nevertheless, the system of co-ordinated subsidies for coal producers represents an element of market management. These subsidies are designed to prevent the coal industry from being displaced, or being displaced unduly rapidly, by cheaper sources of energy such as oil.

The Common Agricultural Policy
The logic of inclusion

First we must ask why such a policy is required at all. The Six could have adopted the approach of the Outer Seven and left agriculture out of the arrangement. However, a programme of economic integration within the Six which excluded agriculture stood no chance of success. It is important to appreciate that the Rome Treaty was a delicate balance of the national interests of the contracting parties. Let us consider West Germany and France in terms of trade outlets. In the case of West Germany the prospect of free trade in industrial goods, and free access to the French market in particular, was extremely inviting. In the case of France the relative efficiency of her agriculture (particularly her grain producers) as compared with West Germany held out the prospect that in a free Community agricultural market she would make substantial inroads into the West German market. This was obviously likely to result if the common price level of grain, for example, was set well below the West German level but at or above the French level. Agriculture had therefore to be included.

These factors do not, however, explain the emergence of a common policy. Agriculture could have been brought within the ambit of the Treaty without resort to common support systems and common price levels. Each member-state could have operated its own agricultural support programme, with protection at the frontier and so forth in order to achieve predetermined price levels. Trade could have been fitted into such a system through the agency of bilateral agreements between members whereby they could have agreed to absorb certain quantities of each other's agricultural output. In practice the Six chose to go further than this since they agreed to free inter-state agricultural trade of all obstacles. This in turn implied uniform prices over the whole Community market. It also gave rise to the establishment of a centralized system for deciding what the common price levels should be and Community machinery for manipulating markets in order to bring them about. A Community system for financing the support policy was also clearly called for. The decision to establish free movement of agricultural goods within the Community was probably the result of two factors. Firstly, anything less than free trade in agriculture would have struck the French as discriminatory when compared with the treatment proposed for industrial goods. Secondly, if trade was not free, and national price levels could differ, then countries with low price levels would enjoy a competitive advantage in so far as low food prices give rise to low industrial wages.

In explaining the inclusion of agriculture within the Rome Treaty some account should also be taken of the sheer size of the agricultural section in 1958. At that time farming occupied fifteen million persons – about 20 per cent of the working population of the Community. A process of economic unification, leading to eventual political integration, could hardly succeed if it failed to address itself to the problems faced by such an important section of the population. Within the Six agriculture is an occupation in which the problem of relatively low incomes is particularly acute. In any case the agricultural vote was so important that agriculture could hardly be ignored.

The system of price support

Although the machinery differs from commodity to commodity, the basic features of the EEC support system are as follows. The income support to producers is guaranteed by manipulating the market so as to bring about a high price – a price which in itself provides an adequate remuneration to farmers. The internal price level is partly maintained by a variety of protective devices at the common frontier. These prevent imports from the low-price world market from eroding the internal price level. But in addition, provision is made for official support buying within the Community so as to take off the market the excess of supply over demand at the predetermined support-price level. The commodities so purchased may be later unloaded on the Community market when demand exceeds supply at the support level. Alternatively, they can be conveyed to other uses. Then again, and this is particularly important, they can be unloaded on the world market, usually at a loss. As already indicated, in broad terms Community policy is a direct descendant of the policies pursued at the national level prior to the signing of the Rome Treaty.

It will immediately be recognized that this approach is the opposite of that adopted in the UK. At the risk of some over-simplification, it can be said that the British approach is to import food at low world prices. (This follows a long tradition in British policy. In the nineteenth century the free-trade policy of the UK involved the exchange of British industrial goods for the primary commodities which the Empire could most efficiently produce. The import of food at low prices found a further expression in the reciprocal Commonwealth Preference system.) In so far as the UK farmer cannot make an adequate living by selling at market prices arising under conditions of free importation, British policy has consisted of granting deficiency payments (financed out of taxation) sufficient to build up the price received by the farmer to a level set out in the Annual Farm Price Review.

A better appreciation of how the Community market support policy works can be derived from considering particular commodities. In the case of grain the Community operates a system of target prices. During the transitional stage the national target prices could and did differ because national markets were protected from each other. However, in 1967 all such protection was swept away and a common target price came into operation. In the case of soft wheat the common target price was DM 425 per ton in the area of greatest deficit in the Community. The latter is defined as the area with the least adequate supplies of soft wheat. The centre chosen was Duisburg in the Ruhr. It was therefore planned to manipulate the market so as to bring about a price of DM 425 at Duisburg. (Target prices in other main marketing centres were established which were essentially regional derivatives of the Duisburg price.)

Intervention prices for grain are set at 5–7 per cent below the target price. When the market price in the Community falls to the intervention price level, support purchases can begin. In this sense the intervention price represents the minimum support price for producers. This system prevents over-production within the Community from pushing the price level down.

In addition, the Community must protect the internal price level from imported supplies. This is done by applying a system of variable levies to supplies emanating from outside the Six. As part of this machinery, a threshold price level is determined. Imported supplies crossing the Community frontier at the threshold price level will, when they bear the further cost of transport, enter market centres at a price equal to the target price set for that centre. If imported supplies cross the frontier below the threshold price, a levy is applied equal to the difference between the price at the frontier and the target price. For example, suppose the target price of grain in the Belgian market centre of Brussels is $105. Suppose also that the cost of transport from Antwerp to Brussels is $5. Then the threshold price at Antwerp is $100. If supplies are imported at Antwerp at a price of $90 then a variable levy of $10 is applied. It should be emphasized that grain is an example of a fairly rigid system of price guarantee. In other cases, for example fruit and vegetables, prices can fall significantly before official support buying begins.

The evolution of policy

Between the signing of the Rome Treaty and 1968, by which time the common price systems had come into operation, the Community achieved three things. Firstly, it dissolved national systems of support. Secondly, the latter were replaced by Community support systems. These were operated during the transitional phase in conjunction with protection between member-states and as a result differences in national price levels continued to exist. Thirdly, the protection between member-states was swept away and thereafter the common support system was accompanied by common prices. The latter are of course agreed annually by the Council of Ministers in the light of proposals submitted by the Brussels Commission.

This evolution has not been achieved without considerable difficulty. Indeed the Community made progress through a series of minor crises. For longish periods the Six failed to resolve their problems. The solution to them was therefore left to marathon sessions of the Council of Ministers during which package deals were evolved. (It might be relevant to add that the ability of the Six to eventually agree was particularly due to the contribution of Sicco Mansholt, the Commissioner who since 1958 has been responsible for agricultural policy.) In December 1961 the Council embarked on a marathon which led to common policies in grains, pig meat, eggs, poultry meat, fruit and vegetables and wine, and to the laying down of the broad principles to be adopted in financing the policy. In December 1963 another marathon dealt with regulations relating to milk and dairy produce, beef and veal, rice and fats. In December 1964 the Council approached the extremely vexed question of the common target price for grain. It ought to be emphasized that progress up to this point had been concerned with support systems and not with the eventual common prices which those systems would produce. The common grain price was essentially the linchpin of the whole system. Once this price was adopted, all the others would tend to fall into place since they all closely linked together. For example, grain is a major input cost in producing poultry, eggs and pig meat. But pig meat and beef prices are related by virtue of competitive substitution. In turn beef prices must stand in a certain relationship to milk prices if the raising of beef and dairy cattle are to be kept in line with evolution of the demand for these two products. The common grain price issue was also important because it brought France and West Germany directly into conflict. Relatively speaking, the West Germans were and still are inefficient producers of wheat when compared with the French. The West Germans were reluctant to agree to a common price which represented a significant fall below their national price level. However, a common price at the German level (it was the highest in the Six in the 1964–65 season) would have done nothing to restrict German output but would have led to a considerable expansion of the output of other producers such as France and the Netherlands. The Community would have had huge grain surpluses on its hands which would have been costly to dispose of on world markets. In addition, since grain is an important input in the agricultural sector, the prices of other agricultural products would have been pushed upwards. The French for their part recognized that a relatively low common grain price would tend to cause a contraction of German grain output and the resulting gap could be filled by French farmers. In the end, after dire threats from the French, the Germans agreed to a common price for soft wheat of DM 245 per ton. This was to be operational from 1 July 1967. This represented a significant cut since the German farm lobby wanted DM 450. As a *quid pro quo* Germany, together with Italy and Luxembourg, received temporary and degressive subsidies from the fund set up to finance the common agricultural policy. Agreement on common prices for other products followed. In the case of milk and dairy products, beef and veal, sugar, rice, oil seeds and olive oil, these were arrived at in another marathon session in July 1966 immediately following the end of the French boycott. It should perhaps be noted that although the common policy is protectionist and does not make sense economically, its creation was a remarkable administrative (and political) achievement. This is all the more true when it is recognized that the system covers about 90 per cent of farm output and the produce of more than ten million operatives.

Grants

In addition to assisting farmers by operating price-support policies, the national governments have given further assistance to farmers in the form of grants. These can be broken down into two kinds – capital and current. The former relates to assistance given to finance the improvement of farm structures, the provision of services such as water and electricity, and the installation of machinery. The latter refer to subsidies to reduce the cost of inputs.

It is obvious that the grant system can undermine the common agricultural policy. Relatively inefficient farms which are in receipt of grants may be enabled to survive whilst more efficient farms which do not receive such financial assistance may have to go out of business. There is indeed much to be said for the view that since price-support systems provide a basis for manipulating the level of farm incomes, current grants at least should be abolished. If they are not to be abolished, then in the interests of creating conditions of undistorted and fair competition there seems to be a good case for harmonization as between states. In the case of capital grants the situation is somewhat different. A uniform system of aids would be nonsense since farms in different areas may have quite different capacities for improvement and the return on capital from such expenditures may therefore differ quite markedly. Given the need to obtain the maximum benefit from the money dispensed on capital grants, and given that capital grants are to continue, there is a case for selectivity.

The Brussels Commission recognizes that such aids constitute a problem and it has compiled an inventory of them which it has broken down into three categories. The first category, which includes assistance to enable holdings to be consolidated, are regarded as beneficial and it is proposed that these should not be made subject to prior notification to the Commission for approval. The second category includes aids which may distort competition in the longer run, but which present no immediate problem. This category includes aids to encourage the purchase of selected seeds and quality animals for breeding. The Commission considers that there may be a need to establish ceilings in the case of such aids but that in due course they may be freed from the need to be notified. The third category is the most important and concerns assistance relating to specific products. Examples include aids to assist the construction of hothouses and buildings to rear pigs and poultry, transport rate subsidies on inter-state shipments and aids for storage which exceed the actual cost involved. These will require prior notification and the Commission intends to propose upper limits in these cases.

Financing the policy

Agricultural policies are apt to cost Governments money. This is undoubtedly true in the case of the UK since, as we have noted, the British system operates to a large extent on the basis of deficiency payments paid for out of tax revenues. At this point it may be worth noting that one reason for not operating a deficiency payments system in the Community was the sheer size of the tax burden which would have been involved.[1] It has also been pointed out that such a system of claims would have been administratively difficult in view of the large number of farmers and the fact that many were poorly educated and some illiterate. But even the common agricultural policy imposes a financial burden on Governments. This arises partly from the fact that the Community has chosen to channel finance into improving the farm structure. The other part of the burden arises from the operation of the system of price and income support. It is not inevitable that a policy based on the EEC model should be a liability to Governments. If a low-price system had been evolved, Community agricultural production would have been held in check. It would not then have been necessary to incur the cost of selling Community surplus production on the world market at a loss. It would also have meant that the Community would have needed to import a substantial proportion of its food requirements and this would have generated a substantial income from variable levies and the like.[2] In practice we shall see that the Community has been driven to pursue a high-price protectionist policy in which the degree of self-sufficiency has tended to increase and which in some cases has led to the Community becoming more than self-sufficient.

When in 1962 the Community established common support systems it also created a new organ for financing the common agricultural policy. This was the European Agricultural Guidance and Guarantee Fund. The Guarantee section deals with the cost arising from support purchases and export refunds. The Guidance section finances structural improvements in farming.

Since 1962/3 the tendency has been for an increasing proportion of the cost of financing the common policy to be borne by the Fund. In 1962/3 the Guarantee section of the Fund reimbursed member-state Governments one-sixth of the relevant expenditure. In 1963/4 this rose to two-sixths and in 1964/5 to three-sixths. In

1. This burden is of course largely psychological. Consumers in the Six pay taxes which are lower than they would be if a deficiency payments system existed, but of course they pay higher market prices for food than would exist under a deficiency payments system.

2. For any given level of imports a low-price system does not of course generate as large a levy income as a high-price system would.

respect of guidance the Fund made available in total a sum equal to about one-third of the money paid out for guarantee purposes. Guidance expenditure took the form of grants to national Governments to cover up to 25 per cent of approved schemes of structural improvement. The Fund itself drew its finance from national exchequers. Whatever sum was required for Fund payments under the guarantee and guidance heads was contributed in certain proportions by the member-states. In 1962/3 the proportions were as for the general budget of the Community – that is West Germany, France and Italy paid 28 per cent each, Belgium and the Netherlands 7·9 per cent, and Luxembourg 0·2 per cent. In 1963/4 and 1964/5 these proportions were progressively changed. A diminishing part of each member-state's liability was determined by the budgetary scale and a rising proportion was provided in relation to each state's net imports of agricultural products from non-member states.

In 1965 the Council of Ministers requested the Commission to produce a plan for financing the common policy for the remaining two years before unified markets began to operate (1967), and also for the period of market unification. Perhaps emboldened by its success in the previous three marathons, and under pressure from some member-state Governments, the Commission chose this as a moment to insert into its proposals measures which were controversial in character. The Commission proposed that all customs duties on intra-Community trade should be abolished by 1 July 1967. Simultaneously, the common external tariff should come into existence. This implied a shortening of the transition period by two-and-a-half years since the Treaty did not require that it should expire until the end of 1969. Since Article 201 of the Rome Treaty provided for the possibility that when the common external tariff was established the proceeds from it should accrue to the Community budget, the Commission proposed that from 1 July 1967 a progressive development should take place in this direction such that by the end of 1977 100 per cent of the customs duties should be paid directly to the Community. In addition, in the light of the decision taken in 1962 by the Council of Ministers that the levies on agricultural imports should accrue directly to the Community when the final stage of the common agricultural policy was reached, the Commission proposed that this provision should also operate from 1 July 1967. Granted that the Community would have a huge income divorced from the control of national parliaments, the Commission saw this as an excellent opportunity to extend the supervisory powers of the European Parliament. If the European Parliament could be given an effective voice over the Community budget, a step would be taken in the direction of a federal Community.

It is of course well known that General de Gaulle found this package very unpalatable. He had no sympathy with the proposal to enhance the power of the European Parliament. Nor did the prospect of a federal budget fed by direct revenues appeal to him. The French therefore decided to boycott the Community, ostensibly because of the failure to agree on new financial provisions by 30 June 1965, but really because of the reasons already referred to. In September 1965 the French President also revealed that he was seeking a revision of the Rome Treaty which would perpetuate the national veto in the Council of Ministers. This was connected with the fact that the Community was about to enter the third stage when most decisions would be made on a majority basis. The subsequent meeting of the Council of Ministers at Luxembourg in January 1966 ended in a twofold agreement. The Five and France agreed to disagree on majority voting. The French agreed to return to the fold.

The return of the French was accompanied by agreement on the method of financing the common agricultural policy for the period up to the end of 1969. The budgetary proportions employed between 1962–3 and 1964–5 were dropped as was the principle of increasingly weighting national contributions according to net imports from non-member states. The proportions for 1965/66 were France 32·58 per cent, West Germany 31·67 per cent, Italy 18 per cent, the Netherlands 9·58 per cent, Belgium 7·95 per cent and Luxembourg 0·2 per cent. (In the 1964 marathon, Italy's contribution for 1965/66 had been reduced to 18 per cent and Germany had for that year agreed to rise above the 31 per cent operating between 1962/63 and 1964/65.) In the year 1966/67 the proportions changed to West Germany 30·83 per cent, France 29·26 per cent, Italy 22 per cent, the Netherlands 9·74 per cent,

Belgium 7·95 per cent and Luxembourg 0·22 per cent. From 1 July 1967 until the end of 1969 the financing method changed. Ninety per cent of all levies, and customs duties, on imports of foodstuffs were handed over by the member-state Governments to the Fund. This was expected to cover about 45 per cent of the Fund's expenditure. The remaining 55 per cent or so was financed by the member-states in the following proportions: France 32·0 per cent, West Germany 31·2 per cent, Italy 20·3 per cent, the Netherlands 8·2 per cent, Belgium 8·1 per cent and Luxembourg 0·2 per cent.

It should be noted that the agreement following the ending of the French boycott did not settle the direct revenue issue. The levies accrued to national exchequers and sums equal to them – but less 10 per cent to cover collection costs – were handed over to the Community chest. It should also be noted that the proposal that the proceeds of the common external tariff should accrue to the Community was tactfully dropped as was the idea of increasing the power of the European Parliament in budgetary matters.

On the expenditure side, from 1 July 1967 the Fund had paid the full cost of expenditure under the guarantee head. However, following the Luxembourg Agreement, West Germany insisted that expenditure on guidance should be limited to $285 million per annum. Capital grants from the guidance section were allotted up to a maximum of 25 per cent (in the case of Luxembourg and Italy up to 45 per cent in certain circumstances) of the total cost of improvement projects provided that the firms involved contributed at least 30 per cent and that some part of the balance was found by the member-state Governments. The new agreement also included certain lump-sum payments to Italy and Belgium to compensate them for the fact that certain common market organizations had not come into operation in accordance with early decisions taken in the Council of Ministers.

The expenditure of the Fund has grown rapidly since 1962/63. In that year the total disbursement on guidance and guarantee was £38 million. In 1969/70 current forecasts put the expenditure at $3124 million. Arising in connexion with this is the question of who has gained and lost through the operation of the Fund. The answer appears to be that, on the basis of experience up to the end of 1968, the main beneficiaries were France and the Netherlands whilst the main losers were West Germany and Belgium. French agricultural output, particularly of grains, has been expanding. France was able to increase its exports of foodstuffs to West Germany from about $170 million in 1960 to about $500 million in 1966 and the process continues. France enjoys the advantage that, as the result of export refunds, even if the extra output has to be dumped on world markets, the price received is still very favourable. Up to the end of 1968 France received more from the Fund than it paid in to the extent of $343 million whilst in the case of West Germany the situation was the reverse to the tune of $324 million (Butterwick and Rolfe, 1968, p. 11). It should be added that the West German position would have been worse had it not been for a once-for-all compensation payment in 1967/68 arising out of the common grain-price agreement.

In 1969 the question of the post-transition period financing of the Agricultural Fund, and indeed the Community's budgetary needs as a whole, fell due for settlement. Issues such as direct revenues and the powers of the European Parliament came to the fore once more. At the Hague summit of December 1969 the French demanded and received satisfaction on the need to quickly devise a financial system for agriculture in the post-transition period. In return the French gave a boost to Community spirit by agreeing to the subsequent opening of negotiations with the four countries who had lodged applications in 1967. Later in December at yet another marathon session the Council of Ministers reached agreement on the financial issue.

The essence of the financial settlement was as follows. As an interim arrangement for 1970 only, the Six agreed to finance the farm policy by making contributions from their budgets – each member-state had to pay a specified 'key' percentage of the cost involved. But from 1971 the Community would have its own direct revenues since member-states would hand over all their receipts from levies and an increasing proportion of their customs duties. By 1975 100 per cent of all levy and customs revenues would be handed over. An administrative rebate of 10 per cent would be allowed. By 1975 the Six will be pooling a levy and customs revenue of about $2200 million. These revenues will, of course, be provided in order to finance the Community budget as a whole and not just agriculture. However, by 1975 the Community budget will probably absorb $4000 million so that there is a significant shortfall which will have to be made good. The latter will be accomplished by a further contribution of up to 1 per cent of the revenue from the then harmonized added value tax – this would raise about $1900 million. Up to 1978 certain safeguards have been built in which set limits to the contributions of each member-state but after 1978 these will cease. The settlement also broke new ground in giving the European Parliament a limited role in budgetary matters.

Farm incomes

Article 39 of the Rome Treaty sets out the objectives of the common agricultural policy. These include the increase of agricultural efficiency, the stability of markets, the guaranteeing of regular supplies and the ensuring of reasonable prices to consumers. The Treaty also refers to the need to ensure a fair standard of living for the agricultural population. Then again, at the time when the foundations of the common agricultural policy were being laid, considerable stress was placed upon the need for a liberal trade policy since if the Community wished to export its own industrial products it had to be prepared to import other countries' agricultural produce. There is of course plenty of scope for conflict here. An obvious way to improve farm incomes is to raise the price of farm produce relative to the cost of producing it. Such a policy would increase farm incomes and provided the price of consumer goods bought by farmers did not rise proportionately their purchasing power would also go up. (In 1958 there was obviously a good case for such a development since farm incomes per head were only 43 per cent of those in the rest of the economy.) But a rise in the price of farm produce conflicts with the consumer's interest in low prices. Also, if a rise in prices stimulates greater home production then there will be less need to import. The latter conflicts with the need to maintain a liberal trade policy. If the Community does not buy from foreigners, why should foreigners buy from the Community?

Perhaps the most interesting of the objectives of the common policy is the one relating to the establishment of a fair standard of living for the agricultural population. This raises the question of what kind of farms are to enjoy this improvement. This was deliberated at length in the early days of the EEC and the Commission decided that the family farm would have a place in the European farm structure provided that it could occupy at least one or two workers full-time.

No policy of improving the relative position of the agricultural population, however, can achieve its end unless there is adequate data about farm incomes. Therefore in 1965 the Council of Ministers adopted a regulation for the purpose of marshalling evidence about agricultural incomes. This takes the form of a Community Farm Accounts Survey. The plan envisages covering 10,000 farms with an eventual build-up to 30,000. The survey will enable the Commission to produce comparative data on incomes in agriculture and industry and will form the main part of a 'Report on the Situation in Agriculture and Agricultural Markets in the Community' which will be addressed to the Council of Ministers and the European Parliament. It is worth noting that this version of the UK Annual Farm Price Review was the result of the 1961–3 UK entry negotiations.

Prospects

Having created this remarkably complex price machinery, the Six are now finding that it is beginning to creak and groan under the pressure of mounting surpluses of agricultural products, particularly butter, grains and sugar. How has this come about? The answer is that the price levels established by the Community have been relatively high. This result has emerged from the bargaining between member-states. In order to achieve agreement the Commission, although initially proposing lower common prices, had subsequently to pitch the price levels well up so that the less efficient could shelter under them. This was clearly the case in milk. The surplus stocks of butter are a direct result of this since the common target price for milk is protected by support purchases of butter. But other factors have also been at work. One is that whereas it was often the case under national systems that price guarantees were limited to a global output quota, the common prices under the common agricultural system apply to total production. The other factor is that as a reward for agreeing to particular aspects of the common policy, member-states have sometimes obtained agreement in the Council of Ministers for a more protectionist regime in respect of products in which they have been particularly interested. For example, Italy obtained this type of concession in respect of fruit and vegetables.

Mounting surpluses are bound to raise the financial requirements of the Fund. A movement towards self-sufficiency or more than self-sufficiency leads to a reduction in revenue from levies on the one hand and an increased expenditure in the form of export refunds on the other. In December 1968, against this background, Sicco Mansholt put forward a new ten-year plan – 'Agriculture 1980'. It is obvious that the disparity between agricultural prices in the Six and the levels obtaining in world markets must be narrowed. The cost of producing food in the Six must be reduced. It also follows that if productivity per man or per acre is to increase, it will be necessary to have fewer men and fewer acres in production if output is to be prevented from outstripping internal needs. It is equally obvious that a policy of improving agricultural incomes by raising prices is likely to be extremely costly. A more acceptable way is to invest money in improving the farm structure. Bigger farms need to be created which will eliminate the concealed unemployment that is characteristic of small farms. Strips need to be consolidated so that time is not lost in proceeding from one plot to another. More mechanization would also help to increase labour productivity. In this way increased incomes could be paid to farmers without increasing the price of agricultural produce.

The Mansholt Plan therefore addresses itself to the task of increasing farm incomes and halting the spiralling cost of the common agricultural policy. To do this it aims to shift the emphasis in the policy from market and price support to structural improvement.

The Commission proposes that farms of a more viable size should be created. The policy should be voluntary. Financial inducements and assistance should be used, but coercion is ruled out. Minimum size units are conceived as being two to three hundred acres for wheat production, forty to sixty cows for milk, and a hundred and fifty to two hundred head of cattle for beef and veal production. This larger size of farm would lead to more efficient use of labour and capital. Given that output must be kept under control, the increase in productivity must be balanced by a reduction in the labour force on the land and by a reduction in the quantity of land devoted to agriculture. Labour is indeed leaving the land but the Commission believes that if the standard of living of those remaining is to increase, the rate at which labour leaves agriculture will have to be increased. If its target is achieved, the actual farm population will fall to 6 per cent of the total working population by 1980; this compares with 20·7 per cent in 1960. As part of its plan of action the Commission is calling for a massive education and retraining programme. The Commission also envisages that by 1980 the farming area in the Community will be reduced from 175 to 160 million acres. It is expected that if the whole programme can be carried through by 1980 then expenditure on supporting prices could fall from the present level of about $2000 million to $750 million.

The French devaluation and German revaluation

Under the common agricultural policy the price of agricultural products is expressed in terms of the Community's unit of account which has a gold content equal to that of the US Dollar. The automatic implication of this is that if a member-state devalues, its farm prices in terms of the national currency rise, and vice versa if it revalues. It has always been a cardinal principle of the policy that the exchange rates of member-states should remain unchanged. However, in August 1969 the French government decided to devalue the Franc by 11·11 per cent. This immediately created a minor crisis, since the common price arrangements were disturbed and there was a danger that French farmers would enjoy an increase in prices whilst farmers in other member-states would not experience any improvement. More important, a rise in French prices would stimulate production and aggravate the already existing surplus problem. A Council meeting was therefore hastily summoned on 11 August. One possibility was that the unit of account could be devalued. However, although this could have offset the effect of devaluation on French producer prices and left them unchanged, it would have automatically worsened the prices received by producers in other member-states. The policy was therefore rejected. Instead, a more complicated arrangement was adopted. During the marketing year 1969–70 the intervention or buying-in prices paid in respect of interventions in the French domestic market were to be reduced by 11·11 per cent with the intention of preventing a rise in prices. The devaluation would also give French food exports a competitive edge whilst imports into France would be disadvantaged. It was therefore decided that France should grant subsidies to imports from member-states and levy compensatory duties on French exports in order not to distort the free movement of agricultural produce. In the 1970–71 period it is apparently intended that intervention prices shall be reduced by 5·5 per cent. Thereafter French agriculture will presumably be re-integrated into the common agricultural policy. The decision to float the German Mark and then revalue it has of course also upset the working of the common policy.

The Common Transport Policy

There are a number of reasons why a common transport policy was called for under the arrangements envisaged by the Rome Treaty. The first is that transport costs are an important factor influencing trade. Since the Community seeks to build up inter-state trade activity it is therefore desirable that there should be a cheap and well co-ordinated Community transport system. As an example of the impact of freight costs we can cite the estimate of the German Railways that in 1957 railway freight charges added 50 per cent to the producer prices of stone and building materials and 9–26 per cent to the prices of bulk goods. In the case of agricultural products it has been estimated that in 1955 in the UK the rail freight charges for a 400 mile journey added 28 per cent to the wholesale price of wheat and 22 per cent to the price of barley and oats. Secondly, it is necessary to recognize that transport on the Continent, as in the UK, has been subjected to considerable state intervention. Since these interventions have not been co-ordinated as between states, considerable distortions could arise. But more important is the fact that transport has been manipulated so as to artificially aid exports and inhibit imports. Experience in the early days of the ECSC indicated that this would also be a problem in a general common market. But there is a third factor. As was indicated earlier in discussing agriculture, the Rome Treaty involved a delicate balance of national interests. In the case of the Netherlands it was clearly anticipated that since transport, particularly that along the Rhine, is a very important contributor to the Dutch GNP, a growth of intra-Community trade would be very advantageous to the Netherlands. It was therefore very obvious from the Dutch point of view that transport should be brought within the ambit of the Treaty and that, in so far as this could be accomplished, member-states should be prevented from hiving transport activity off as a sphere where national interests would predominate. It is perhaps worth noting that in 1963 66·6 million tons of freight was carried to or from the Netherlands along the Rhine, a large part of this trade being transit in character. This constituted 61 per cent of all Rhine traffic, and 53 per cent of it was carried under the Dutch flag.

The Commission's blueprint

The Rome Treaty itself is remarkably uninstructive on the nature of the common policy. It was left to the Brussels Commission to provide a basis for such a policy. In 1961 the Commission produced a memorandum which laid down what it thought should be the general principles of the common transport policy – this was known as the Schaus Memorandum (EEC Commission, 1961) after Lambert Schaus who was the Commissioner responsible for transport affairs. Then in 1962 the Commission produced its Action Programme (EEC Commission, 1962) which reviewed the measures which the Commission proposed should be implemented. The memorandum outlined three main objectives which the policy should achieve. One was to remove obstacles which transport could put in the way of a general common market. Another was that the policy should not merely aim to sweep away factors which delayed the creation of a common market, but should be a powerful stimulant to the growth of trade and the

opening up of national markets. Both these were generally acceptable. The third was much more controversial. The Commission
suggested that the Community should 'endeavour to create
healthy competition of the widest scope'. In the light of the highly
regulated nature of transport within the Community this was
bound to be a controversial proposition, all the more so as the
Commission proposed that the common transport policy should
apply to national as well as international transport activity.

In working towards a basically competitive solution, the Commission had to deal with the fact that national authorities, in
varying degrees, exerted two general kinds of control over transport activity. One was control over rates. The other was a quantitative control through the agency of licensing and quotas. The
Commission took the view that a more flexible price system would
have to operate in which enterprises would be free to operate on
the basis of commercial criteria. This also implied powers to close
down services if necessary. The Commission's proposal was that
the Community should adopt a rate bracket or fork-tariff system.
This was to apply to road, rail and inland waterway transport,
whether national or international. Provision was also to be made
for rate publicity. Own-account transport, as opposed to that for
hire and reward, was to be exempt. Under this system the relevant
authorities would specify maximum and minimum rates for
particular types of traffic on the various routes, and consignors
and carriers would be able to negotiate rates anywhere within
the spread. The apparent logic of the arrangement was that the
upper limit was designed to prevent monopolistic exploitation.
The lower limit was designed to prevent the deterimental effects of
excessive competition. The latter point requires some elucidica-
tion. Apparently, what the Commission thought was as follows.
Freight transport is subject to undesirable rate fluctuations. This
is due to marked inelasticities on both the demand and supply
sides. Demand for transport depends on the general level of
activity and in the short-term a fall in rates will not stimulate an
extension of demand. On the supply side, because of the small-
scale nature of much of the entrepreneurship, a fall in rates
will not lead to a contraction of supply. Supply may indeed
behave perversely in that vehicle owners may, when rates fall,

seek to maintain their incomes by working longer hours. In so far as such conditions exist, a fall in demand would undoubtedly precipitate a steep fall in rates. Allied to all this is the fact that in a boom large numbers of new entrants may be attracted into the transport industry. This will be particularly the case in road haulage where capital requirements are relatively small. In a subsequent slump, however, capacity may not contract quickly. Instead entrepreneurs may for a significant period of time be prepared to accept rates which cover direct costs and make some small contribution to overheads. Under such circumstances rates may be dragged down for a substantial period. Such conditions may have a deleterious effect on investment in the industry and on road safety.

However, this argument is not wholly convincing. In the first place it seems possible that the adoption of the rate-bracket system was based not so much on economic considerations as on the need to achieve a compromise between the relatively free rate system required by the Dutch and the rigid fixed-rate system which had been operational in West Germany. On the economic plane a number of criticisms can be raised. The first relates to the proneness of transport rates to marked fluctuations. More empirical evidence is needed here. It should be added that national experience indicates that the Commission's fears are not wholly justified. Secondly, as the Allais Report on transport pricing pointed out, there is much to be said for setting transport rates free and seeing what will happen. If monopoly or ruinous price cutting occurs, maximum and minimum brackets can be applied as and when required. It is in any case difficult to justify the simultaneous application of maximum and minimum rates (EEC Commission, 1965). This implies that monopolistic exploitation and ruinous price wars are likely to occur at one and the same time on a particular route! There is a third factor which should inhibit transport authorities from operating a rate-bracket system and that is the sheer magnitude of the administrative task involved. The costing effort called for is immense. This in turn gives rise to suspicion that the brackets will not be determined in any very scientific fashion. Rather, where a fixed rate already exists brackets may be set around it. Then again, where freer rates exist and the industry regards the going rate as adequate, the brackets may be set with reference to that figure.

The argument for calling transport a managed market partly arises from the administrative limits set to rate fluctuations by the brackets. How far in practice the Community solution is a managed one will depend on how much transport activity is placed under the rate-bracket regime and how wide the spread is between the brackets. If the brackets are sufficiently wide apart they may rarely exercise an influence.

Having proposed a system in which pricing freedom and competition between the various modes of transport would have a role to play, the Commission recognized that competition would not work in an undistorted fashion unless as between the member-states there was harmonization of the fiscal, technical and social burdens placed upon transport. Also, competition between the different forms of transport could not lead to the best use of resources unless action was taken to ascertain the costs of infrastructure, i.e. track costs, and an attempt was made to allocate these costs among the beneficiaries. The stress on a commercial approach to transport policy also required that where possible enterprises should be financially independent and should seek to balance their accounts without resort to state subsidies. If enterprises are burdened with such social obligations they should be compensated for the extra costs, and if they enjoy certain privileges they should pay for them. This latter process is termed normalization of accounts.

The second main area where the Commission has seen the need for change is licensing and quotas. Since this is a large problem we shall confine the discussion to the quantitative aspects of road transport. Let us consider the international aspect first. In respect of own-account transport the Commission took the view that there should be complete liberalization. This would imply that producers could carry their own products in their own vehicles anywhere in the Community and that no member-state should be able to set a limit to the number of such foreign vehicles that could be admitted to its territory. In respect of hire and reward vehicles, however, the Commission's original proposals were more complicated. This form of transport has been governed by agreements between the administrative authorities of member-states. They have been typically bilateral in character in that each state has laid down the number and load capacity of vehicles from the other state which it would allow on its territory at any one time. Broadly speaking, the Commission concluded that the quotas had not been expanded to the extent corresponding to the growth of trade between the member-states concerned. The Commission therefore proposed, firstly, that bilateral quotas should be enlarged in conformity with the growth of inter-state trade. Secondly, that the bilateral licences should be progressively faded out. As the bilateral licences disappeared the Community licences would come into existence at a rate sufficient (a) to compensate for the disappearance of the bilateral licences, and (b) to cope with the growth of intra-Community trade. The new body of licences was to be termed the Community Quota. A French holder of such a licence could, for example, carry a load from Paris to Brussels. At Brussels he could discharge his load and take on another for Duisburg, and at Duisburg he could take on goods for Milan, and so forth.

In the case of national road transport for hire and reward the Commission recognized that all member-states limited entry by licensing. The Commission did not propose to eliminate the licensing system and to that extent it implied that a management element would continue. The Action Programme did, however, propose a harmonization and modification of national licensing practices. The modification would be designed to increase the flexibility of national licensing systems. In practice the Commission held the view that licence-quota policy had been restrictive and had given rise to relatively high rates.

Three further aspects of the transport policy require mention. The first is that Article 7 of the Rome Treaty requires that there shall be no discrimination on grounds of nationality, and in Article 79 this is reiterated in the case of transport. Secondly, we have already referred to the Rome Treaty's attack on state aids, and Article 80 reiterates this by prohibiting support rates. The latter are favourable transport rates designed to assist particular enterprises or industries (there are, however, exceptions to the prohibition of support rates). Thirdly, the Commission deems it important that there shall be some co-ordination of national transport network planning. In other words, it is desirable that member-states constructing motorways to the same stretch of a common frontier should not end up with the roads terminating five miles apart!

Policy achievements

Progress in constructing a common policy in transport has been slow, particularly when compared with the vast achievements in agriculture. One of the first developments was the promulgation in 1960 of a Regulation relating to the prohibition of discrimination. This began to take effect on 1 July 1961. The ban on support tariffs came into effect in January 1962 with the entry into the second stage of the transition period. The Commission has, as part of its day-to-day activity, been exercising a continuous supervision over transport rates in order to enforce Articles 79 and 80. It is also relevant to mention the right of establishment which means, for example, that a firm in one member-state can set up in the road transport business in another. A firm so setting up would of course have to face the fact that licences are not freely available on request.

In 1964 the Council of Ministers also issued a Regulation relating to infrastructure costs. This provided for an enquiry relating to the year 1966. The Regulation required that the Commission should submit to the Council of Ministers a report together with a study of the way infrastructure costs were met and proposals for a uniform system of assessing and distributing them.

In the case of own-account road transport, when the Commission came to review the situation, it found national road transport arrangements were fairly close to what it desired. In the case of international own-account activity, the situation was from the beginning relatively liberal and in 1964 the Commission was able to secure the Council of Ministers' approval to complete liberalization. Also in 1964 the Council of Ministers reached agreement on a Community Quota. The basis of the agreement was that the Community Quota and the adaptation of bilateral quotas were to come into operation on 1 January 1966. The Community Quota was to operate for the four years 1966 to 1969 and this was to be an experimental period. The quota for 1966 was to consist of 880 authorizations divided as follows: West Germany 210, France 210, the Netherlands 176, Belgium 118, Italy 142 and Luxembourg 42. The division of the total quota for the years 1967–9 was to be decided subsequently. Criteria to be applied in apportioning the licences included the development of trade and the use made of the authorizations. No state would suffer an absolute fall in its allocation. Simultaneously with the establishment of the Community Quota, existing bilateral quotas would be adapted to transport needs by means of negotiations between member-states. No actual Council Regulation emerged as a result of this accord, since the agreement of the French was contingent upon a solution being found to the rate-bracket issue. Before leaving this subject we might mention that the Community Quota agreement departed from the Commission's original proposals in a number of ways. One was that whereas the Commission envisaged the disappearance of the bilateral quotas, the 1964 accord envisaged their retention and adaptation to current needs. The Community content was therefore whittled down.

In 1965 the Council also reached agreement on tariffication and thus appeared to bring to an end a long period of stalemate. The French abandoned the principle that tariff brackets should be applied to all forms of transport and the Dutch agreed to a system of publicity. The agreement was as follows. During stage one, which it was proposed would last for three years from 1 January 1967, the rate-bracket system would apply to international transport only. There would in fact be two forms of rate-bracket system – compulsory and reference. International road traffic, that is, for journeys of more than fifty kilometers, would come under the compulsory system. The latter system would also apply to international rail transport. In respect of rail traffic, however, it would be possible to conclude special contracts where these were required to counter competition from other transport media. For international inland waterway traffic, on the other hand, the reference system would apply. The reference bracket was so called because it would serve as a guide to enterprises as to the rates they ought to charge. It would not, however, be compulsory to charge rates equal to or within the brackets. If enterprises charged rates

outside the brackets details would have to be published, whereas
if they charged rates within the brackets no publication would be
required. Both compulsory and reference brackets were to be
published. In stage two, which would last from 1 January 1969 to
1 January 1972, the bracket system would be applied to domestic
transport as well. The arrangements for international traffic
would be the same as in stage one, with the important difference
that the reference-rate system would be applicable to heavy
merchandise. For the rest of domestic transport, member-states
would be able to choose between the compulsory and reference
systems. The publicity arrangements would continue to apply.
During the final stage, beginning in 1972, the whole system of rate
brackets would be reviewed.

Ironically, this agreement was concluded just before the French
decided to boycott the Community. No formal regulation therefore emerged, and as a result the accord on the Community Quota
was not implemented either. But the return of the French did not
lead to progress. The discussion of details arising out of the 1965
agreement lead to deadlock, mainly because of continuing differences between the Six on the degree of market regulation required.
The Dutch wished to see a more liberal regime than some of the
other member-states. However, in December 1967 the Council
met and decided that the stalemate could not continue any longer.
It decided that regulations covering important areas of policy
should be agreed by mid-1968. The Council was probably gal-
vanized into activity by signs that at least one member-state was
proposing to take action which was likely to create even greater
divergences between national policies. Late in 1967 the West
German Government published the Leber Plan which was aimed
at reducing road congestion and drastically reducing the German
railway deficit. In January 1968 the Commission urged the West
German Government to modify the plan. In particular the Commission considered that the proposed tax on road haulage and the
ban on the road carriage of certain goods should be abandoned.

In July 1968 the Council adopted a series of regulations. One
related to the Community Quota, or Community Passport as it is
now called. The Council agreed that up to the end of 1971 1200
Community licences should be issued. These licences will be

divided as follows: West Germany 286, France 286, the Netherlands 240, Italy 194, Belgium 161 and Luxembourg 33. Secondly, the Council adopted a regulation introducing a tariff-bracket system for international road transport. The appropriate authorities will publish fixed upper and lower brackets with a maximum spread of 23 per cent below the ceiling level. Goods must be carried at these rates. Private contracts may be concluded outside the published brackets. These private contracts, which must be immediately notified to the authorities, may be concluded for limited periods of time for consignments exceeding 500 metric tons per three months. Competitive conditions must exist. If there is a disturbance in the transport market all private contacts may, for a set period, require the prior approval of the authorities. The system will apply up to the end of 1971 but can be extended by one year if no agreement is forthcoming in 1971 about the system which will follow.

Regulations have also been adopted in the field of harmonization. One relates to tax-free entry of fuel in vehicle tanks. The other relates to conditions of employment of lorry drivers and specifies the age of drivers in relation to the size of vehicles, as well as maximum driving hours, and rest periods.

The Council also declared that the rules of competition contained in Articles 85 and 86 should apply to transport. (From 1962 until 1968, despite the Commission's view that the competition rules applied to transport, the Council refused to bring such activity within the ambit of the anti-trust rules.) In line with the Treaty, the Council regulation envisages situations in which agreements can be permitted. For example, agreements may be upheld if they bring stability to markets subject to major fluctuations.

In 1969 the Council took a further step towards establishing a common policy. It adopted a regulation providing for the normalization of railway accounts under common rules for the granting of subsidies. The Council also decided that some categories of subsidy should be progressively eliminated. The Ministers also agreed on a common definition of the obligations that Governments could impose on road, rail and inland waterway transport in return for subsidies.

It is thus apparent that in 1968 the Six began to make progress towards a common policy. But it is equally evident, in the light of the list of measures envisaged by the Commission in 1961 and 1962, that much yet remains to be achieved.

The Common Energy Policy

Progress in this field has been limited. There are three reasons for this. Firstly, the responsibility for energy matters has been a divided one. The Paris Treaty placed responsibility for coal fairly and squarely on the shoulders of the ECSC. The Rome Treaty established that oil, natural gas, hydro-power and electric current were the province of the EEC. The task of dealing with nuclear power was assigned to Euratom. Secondly, none of the three Treaties contains a word about a common energy policy or even lays down a timetable for its elaboration. In some degree this fact is a reflection of the circumstances of the time when the Treaties were drafted. They all belong to the period when coal was the major source of energy in the Six. (In 1950 it met almost 75 per cent of the primary energy needs of the Community.) The main problem then was guaranteeing that the supply of coal was available, firstly on non-discriminatory terms to all Community purchasers, and secondly at reasonable prices. The latter meant the Six had to address themselves to the problems of the coal cartels, in particular the Ruhr cartels of which Georg was the most notorious. The decline of coal, the emergence of associated regional difficulties, together with the growing dependence on imported sources of energy, were problems of the future and were not then foreseen. The third reason for lack of progress is the involved nature of the problem. Governments, even in liberal economies, tend to get caught up in regulating the energy market. The Six were and are no exception – the regional problem, state monopolies, nationalized undertakings and fiscal policy are just a few of the complicating elements.

The necessity for a common policy: arguments and issues

One of the most frequently quoted arguments relates to the distortions which arise in the absence of such a policy. National energy policies exhibit significant differences and these affect the price of energy in national markets. For example, member-states have differed in the taxes which they have imposed on fuel oil and in respect of the tariffs and quota arrangements for imported coal. Because energy consititutes a significant proportion of the total cost of producing some goods, these differences can and do lead to serious distortions of the competitive process. An illustration of the possibility of distortion is provided by the fact that in steel production direct and indirect energy procurements constitute 26 per cent of the total value of the product. In chemicals, non-ferrous metals, transport and building materials (including glass), the figures are 16, 15, 14 and 12 per cent respectively (ECSC, 1967, p. 11).

The second reason for a Community policy is connected with the increased competition which coal has been encountering, particularly from oil. This has thrown up a series of issues including unemployment and regional decline, the problem of the security and stability of energy supplies as the Community becomes steadily more dependent on imported sources, and the likely long-term evolution of the price of imported energy sources.

An appreciation of this set of interrelated issues requires that we go back in time to the first half of the 1950s. In this period there was a coal shortage, which in turn prompted users to do two things. They sought to economize in the use of coal; for example, the steel industry succeeded in developing techniques which curtailed heat losses. They also began to turn to substitutes – in practice this usually meant oil. However, this tendency to take decisions against coal was masked by the rapid economic growth of the period. Indeed, when in 1956 the OEEC produced the Hartley Report (*Europe's Growing Needs of Energy – How Can They Be Met?*), the essential message was that there was a danger of a possible shortage of energy in Europe. Stress was also laid on the balance-of-payments problems inherent in dependence on imported energy. The Suez crisis appeared to vindicate this view since the immediate effect was rising prices stemming from high ocean freight rates for imported oil and coal. But the picture soon changed. The major oil companies, in order to cope with the growing demand, embarked on a programme of expanded production. They also began to diversify the areas in which they were prospecting and in so doing discovered substantial new reserves. In addition, the majors were joined by new companies who sought to carve out a place for themselves in the world market by offering low prices. The US Government also played a part. In order to protect the home market it applied import quotas and as a result the bulk of the increased supplies flowed to markets such as Western Europe. Moreover, the Soviet Government decided during this period to resume selling Russian oil in the world market. Then again, imported oil gained the advantage of lower freight rates arising from major economies in transportation as a result of the use of bigger and faster ships.

The result of all this was that coal's competitive position deteriorated drastically. After 1956 the price of oil fell and there after stayed low, whereas the price of domestically produced coal (despite a great increase in mechanization and in output per man-shift) climbed steadily upwards. The position in 1956 and 1965 is shown in Table 5.

Table 5

Comparative Price Movements of Imported Coal and Oil and Community Coal ($ Per Ton)

	Community coal*	Imported US coal†	Imported crude oil‡
1956	12·53	21·60	20·30
1965	16·68	14·20	16·40

* Ruhr bituminous (schedule ex-mine).
† American coking fines c.i.f. Amsterdam/Rotterdam/Antwerp.
‡ Kuwait crude c.i.f. Naples.
Source: European Coal and Steel Community (1967, pp. 27–8).

The effect of oil (and natural gas) on coal's position has been dramatic. As we have indicated, coal was responsible for almost three-quarters of the Community's primary energy supplies in 1950 and petroleum contributed 10 per cent. By 1966 coal had fallen to 38 per cent and petroleum had risen to 45 per cent. The rapid rise in the energy requirements of the Community has been met by oil, whereas between 1957 and 1966 coal production fell by 12 per cent, the mining labour force below ground fell by 24 per cent and the number of pits in operation by 42 per cent.

This evolution has presented the Community with three main problems. Firstly, there was the resulting unemployment. The problem would not be so difficult if the employment in coal mining was evenly spread; unfortunately it is concentrated in pockets and this gives rise to the threat of a severe regional problem. The unemployment problem would of course be more tractable if the rate of decline of coal was even merely arrested. Secondly, there was the fact that unlike other major economic blocs (the USSR and USA), the Community is highly dependent on imported supplies of energy and is becoming more so. This raises the question of the stability and security of supplies. If there were a major political upheaval in areas mainly responsible for the supply of energy to the Community the consequences could be disastrous. The need for security and stability of supplies provides an argument for supporting indigenous sources. There are, of course, other approaches to the problem such as stockpiling oil and diversifying oil supplies. (Indeed, the discovery of natural gas is helping to alleviate this problem.) Thirdly, there was the question of the long-term evolution of the world energy market. In 1962 the West European coal producers and the National Coal Board produced a memorandum (*Meeting Europe's Energy Requirements*) which argued that by the mid-1970s there would be a world shortage of energy and that in this light the prices ruling in the early 1960s were only temporarily low. They argued that it would therefore be prudent to keep mines in production. Subsidies would be required in the short term but in the longer term the energy price-level would rise and coal mining would become economic. There could be no question of closing the mines down in the short run and opening them up later since mining communities would have dispersed and the source of labour would be lost for ever. Also the mines would flood and the cost of bringing them back into production would be extremely high. Sinking new pits would be extremely costly, and it has to be borne in mind that there could be a gap of ten to fifteen years between starting to sink a pit and reaching a high rate of production.

A common energy policy: the first steps

In 1964 the ECSC took the first step along the road to a common energy policy when the Council of Ministers formally adopted the Protocol of Agreement on energy policy. This laid down certain broad objectives – cheapness of supply, security of supply, fair conditions of competition among the different sources of energy, and freedom of choice for consumers. The Protocol did not generally lay down details of policy but in the case of coal it did call for the speedy implementation of a co-ordinated system of state aids or subsidies. It is perhaps worth noting that in the case of coal the Community chose subsidies whereas in agriculture the task of rendering Community production profitable was achieved by a different route. In other words, it was decided that coal would be rendered competitive not by raising the price of imported oil to meet the price of coal but by enabling Community producers to supply their output at a price less than would otherwise be the case. The Community has indeed opted for a low-cost energy policy. There can be no doubt that this was the easiest path to pursue. Firstly, the Community was merely recognizing what was already happening, namely that as coal felt the impact of the competition from oil member-states were, in the interests of security and regional policy, granting their collieries half-concealed subsidies. The Protocol was therefore an open recognition of what had been happening anyway. Secondly, states such as Italy, which relied heavily on imported oil, would have strongly resisted any policy which raised their industrial costs.

It will therefore be appreciated that the Protocol envisaged a Community system of state aids or subsidies to the coal mines. This implied some co-ordination. Since subsidies were explicitly forbidden by the Paris Treaty it also required the invoking of Article 95 which allowed the High Authority to take special decisions 'in all cases not expressly provided for in the Treaty' when this appeared 'necessary to fulfill one of the Objectives of the Community'. The basic principle of co-ordination was that measures of aid by member-states should be scrutinized by the High Authority. The latter would have the power to authorize them on the basis of Community criteria. These criteria included assessment of the degree to which the aids enabled the mines to adjust to the new market situation, the degree to which they assisted in preventing unemployment and economic disturbance and the degree to which competitive behaviour between mines was distorted. In particular, the High Authority had to direct its scrutiny towards two kinds of aids. One was contributions towards the social security costs of mining firms. This change in the manpower situation had led to these becoming excessive and the High Authority had to ensure that assistance did no more than defray the abnormal costs of social security and did not act as a positive subsidy which would put some mines at an advantage as compared with others. The other kind of aid was that made available for rationalization. The High Authority was given the power to authorize such subsidies in so far as they enabled mines to adjust to the new market conditions and did not distort competition between mines. Rationalization aid could take the form of assistance to enable mines to be closed, to improve the efficiency and productivity of mining enterprises and to help meet the cost of recruitment, training and retraining. The possibility was also envisaged that mining areas might be so badly affected by the competition from oil that serious disturbances were possible. In such cases extra aid was possible.

Two points are worthy of note. Firstly, although a Community aid system was envisaged this did not extend to Community financing. The cost of subsidies was to be borne by national exchequers. It could be argued that Community finance was appropriate. For example, in so far as keeping coal mines in production is dictated by the security-of-supply argument, why should Italy be able to enjoy the advantage of cheap oil imports and be allowed to avoid the cost of coal subsidies and yet be able to turn back to coal on non-discriminatory terms if oil supplies became inadequate or oil prices rose steeply? The second point is that at no time did the Council of Ministers take a decision on the amount of coal which was to be kept in production. However, the High Authority did in 1966 propose that the Community should guarantee outlets for 190 million tons of coal in 1970. By so doing the Community would keep the proportion of energy requirements met from Community sources close to 50 per cent. One way of doing this was to place quantitative restrictions on coal imports. Another was to subsidize domestic coal used by the iron and steel industry.

In 1966, however, a Community element did creep into the subsidy system. This arose in connexion with coking coal. The impetus for this move were the difficulties arising from the import of cheap American coal. Because there is no common external tariff or common commercial policy under the Paris Treaty, member-states are free to protect their coal industries, or alternatively to import coal at world prices. To the extent that member-states tended to import American coal two effects were apparent. One was that countries such as the Netherlands and Italy which had sited their steel plants on the coast were in a good position to take advantage of these cheap supplies. On the other hand, West German iron and steel enterprises were highly dependent on the higher-priced domestic supplies. This distorted conditions of competition within the Community iron and steel market. The other effect was that cheap imported coal contributed towards a further erosion of the position of Community coal producers. The High Authority therefore proposed a subsidy for Community coking coal and coke. It was argued in justification that if no subsidy were given intra-Community imports would dry up as industry switched to imported supplies, and that the subsidy would help to buttress the domestic industry. Opposition was encountered from the French but in 1967 the Council of Ministers agreed to a subsidy system. Where coking coal and furnace coke produced in a particular member-state was delivered to the steel industry of that state, the subsidies would be paid by the member-state Government concerned. For coking coal and coke entering into intra-Community trade the subsidies (which were to be limited in size) were to be financed from two sources. The producing country had to meet 40 per cent of the cost; the other 60 per cent was borne by a common fund. The Six contributed to the latter as follows: West Germany 28 per cent, France 28 per cent, Italy 14 per cent, Belgium 11 per cent, the Netherlands 10 per cent and Luxembourg 9 per cent. The ceiling for subsidies on intra-Community trade was to be twenty-two million units of account.

The 1968 initiative

In December 1968 the new fourteen-man Commission presented a memorandum to the Council of Ministers entitled 'First guide lines for a Community energy policy' (EEC Commission, 1968a). This was an attempt to put new impetus behind the search for a common policy. The document is extremely detailed and the following description should be taken as an account only of its most striking features. The policy seeks to achieve the same aims as the Protocol. Apart from freedom of choice for consumers and fair competition between energy suppliers, the essential aims are stability, security and cheapness of supplies. The memorandum implicitly admits that up to a point there is some conflict between these latter aims.

The Commission recognizes the existence of distortions. It therefore proposes that the solution to this problem is the full implementation of the Rome Treaty in the energy field. Within the Community freedom of movement of supplies must be achieved. This means the elimination of impediments, whether they be state monopolies or technical obstacles. Differences in taxes are a distorting factor. The specific solutions are the harmonization of the tax on value added in the energy sector, the harmonization of specific consumer taxes on energy products and the harmonization of taxes on hydro-carbon fuel in conjunction with the elaboration of the common transport policy. Whilst on the subject of the full establishment of the common market in the energy sector, we might note that the Commission calls for the full implementation of freedom of establishment and freedom to supply services.

Security of supplies calls for action in a number of energy fields, particularly coal and oil. The memorandum recognizes that the domestic coal production necessary to ensure security cannot be achieved without a co-ordinated import policy. In the light of the past High Authority pronouncements this could be interpreted to mean that the Community should have a common commercial policy which sets quantitative limits to coal imports. The memorandum recognizes the need for aids to the coal mines. It is, however, also recognized that production should be concentrated on the most efficient mines. The memorandum calls for the introduction of Community aid arrangements. Since Community co-ordination already exists this could refer to the need for Community financing. The Commission also calls for better co-ordination of existing Community aid with national aids. In the field of oil, adequate stockpiles is one way to achieve security and in 1968 the Council of Ministers agreed that each member-state should maintain stocks equal to sixty-five days' consumption. National Governments, and not the Commission, can commandeer these stocks if a crisis arises. The memorandum also calls for a Community supply policy and a Community supply programme. Undoubtedly the intention here is that the Community should watch the pattern of oil imports in order to guarantee that it is sufficiently diversified. If the Community is not satisfied with the pattern, the memorandum proposes that suitable procedures for remedying the situation should be evolved. The Community should also be constantly considering the supply possibilities open to the Community, the risks of interruption and the methods of coping therewith.

The Commission also proposes that the ECSC principle of drawing up general objectives (i.e. forecasts of the evolution of demand) should be applied not only to coal but to the whole of the energy sector, particularly in order to guarantee that investment keeps pace with the rapidly rising demand for energy. The ECSC principle of notification of investment projects (which has been operational since the Paris Treaty in respect of coal and steel) should also be generally applicable in the energy sector. Opinions should be rendered on investment projects, and Community control procedures could be elaborated if experience showed that recommendations were being ignored.

The Commission also recognizes the need to maintain competition in energy supply. Since some enterprises already occupy a dominant position in the market for oil, natural gas and nuclear fuels, the Commission proposes that there should be a notification system, together with a period of suspension of action, where mergers are contemplated. This will enable the Commission to render an opinion. The possibility of preventive control is contemplated in this field. The Commission also suggests *a posteriori* notification of the prices obtaining in the market for energy. This is no doubt particularly intended to put the oil industry on a par with the coal industry which, under the Paris Treaty, has been required to publish its price lists.

6 Regional and Social Policy

When drafting the Rome Treaty, the authors were aware that merely to create a regime of intensified competition would not suffice. And within national economies it is recognized that policies are necessary to deal with the problems created when new industries replace old ones (particularly if the latter are large and geographically concentrated) and when more favoured regions forge ahead while the less favoured decline. Likewise, on the Community plane regional and social policy instruments have been devised in order to cope with the problems which ultimately stem from intensified competition across national boundaries.

Regional Policy
Economic integration and the regional problem

It has been repeatedly stressed that the EEC was conceived as being the forerunner of political unity among the Six at least. It is not difficult to see that such unity would be severely jeopardized if the economic policy of the Community did not tackle the problem of the disparities in income per head as between the member-states and as between regions within member-states. To put it another way, the success of the Community as a durable political entity could not be guaranteed if the arrangement was seen as benefiting some states or areas at the expense, or to the exclusion, of others. The latter point gathers added force when it is remembered that economic difficulties could be accentuated by political, linguistic, cultural and religious divisions. Economic differences could then fan the flames of separatism based on these latter factors. This in turn leads us to consider the effects which economic integration has on regional disparities. It is necessary to ask the following questions, in particular. Could the creation of the Common Market create new regional problems and also aggravate those regional disparities which are already in existence?

One possible source of regional difficulty could be the effects of competition. One of the anticipated effects of the creation of the

Common Market is that it would stimulate greater efficiency, in that the more efficient enterprises would expand and the less efficient would contract. It is not inevitable that this would contribute to an aggravated regional problem in one state. A state might find one of its industries succumbing to international competition. But equally well there is no *a priori* reason not to expect that it might have one or more industries which are simultaneously under the influence of the new opportunities created by the Common Market. Labour from the contracting industry would then move into the expanding industry or industries. Moreover, output per head in expanding industry, particularly if it was a new one, might exceed ouptut per head in the contracting industry, particularly if it was an old one. Employment prospects might therefore remain unchanged and income per head could rise. However, all this is based upon a number of assumptions which do not always hold. Industries are sometimes geographically concentrated either because of the existence of local supplies of raw materials and fuel or because of the external economies to which geographical concentration gives rise. Labour would therefore have to move to get new jobs and it has to be remembered that labour is not always highly mobile. Then again the unemployed labour force might be unskilled and unadaptable.

The classic case of the decline of a geographically concentrated industry within the Community as a result of competition is that of Belgian coal. The Belgian industry is divided into two zones, the Campine Basin in the north and the Southern Basin which is an extension of the French Nord/Pas-de-Calais field. The Southern Basin – the more important of the two – was particularly inefficient owing to a combination of poor geological conditions, old equipment and small pits. The pits of the Borinage were the most inefficient of all. Some indication of the inefficiency of the Southern Basin can be derived from the fact that in 1950 the output per man-shift (in kilogrammes) was 1075 whereas in the Ruhr, Saar and Lorraine the figures were 1486, 1676 and 2088 respectively. The Belgian coal industry was of course an extremely important source of employment. Not only did 10 per cent of the Belgian industrial labour force find employment in the industry but that employment was naturally concentrated on the coal fields. The decline in the fortunes of coal, particularly in the face of oil imports, therefore posed a grave regional problem for Belgium. Inevitably, if the Community coal industry had to contract, it was the high-cost sector which was most likely to bear the brunt. This is indeed what happened. Whereas between 1956 and 1966 German and French output fell by 16 per cent and 9 per cent respectively, Belgian output fell by 41 per cent. This development was somewhat ironic. Traditionally the problem area of Belgium was Flanders where agriculture was the predominant occupation and incomes relatively low. The Wolloon area on the other hand enjoyed a prosperity founded on coal and steel. But as a result of the decline of coal the Wolloon area suffered a setback whilst new industries moved into the Flemish region and greatly improved the local income levels. The fact that as between these regions there were and still are deep tensions based on religion, language and culture should not go unnoticed.

It is of course necessary to keep in perspective the effect of the new competition stemming from the creation of the Common Market. There is reason to believe that it is a medium-term rather than a long-term factor. The customs union has after all been created, and previously protected sectors have already been exposed to competition. On the other hand we have to recognize that the decline of an inefficient industry may be a long-drawn-out process. It is also possible that inefficient industries may be protected by non-tariff barriers and that a decline will only really ensue when these are eliminated. (Industries will of course decline in the future but this will be due to technological progress and changes in the structure of demand and not to the reduction of protective barriers.)

A second way in which regional difficulties could arise out of economic integration is connected with factor price equalization. As we have already noted the EEC in principle calls for the free movement of factors of production. In so far as this exists there is bound to be a tendency for the earnings of factors to be equalized as between states much in the same way that this takes place within states. Thus capital would tend to flow from areas where its remuneration was low to where its remuneration was high, and vice versa, until differences were eliminated. Labour, though much less mobile, might be expected to tend to do likewise. But in the case of labour factors other than pure market forces might also operate. For example, just as within states we tend to find national rather than regional wage rates and bargaining, so in the Community there could be a tendency for wage rates to be equalized as between states through the comparability principle. (In the UK we already see this factor at work in respect of airline pilots' pay.) In so far as such equalization tends to take place, it has been argued that the earnings of capital and labour will approximate to what the most productive industries can pay. Whereas enterprises at the centre, where production conditions are favourable, will be able to pay the equalized rate, enterprises in the peripheral areas, away from the centres of population and sources of raw material, will find that costs of production are relatively high and they will not be able to pay the rate. As a result unless firms located in the peripheral areas receive subsidies, the industries located there will tend to decline.

There is a further series of factors which may perhaps be more important. A glance at the map of the Six quickly reveals that the most highly developed regions form a bloc of concentrated economic activity centred on the Rhine–Rhone axis extending from the Netherlands in the north to Northern Italy in the south. In 1963 the Birkelbach Report to the European Parliament estimated that this area covered about 35 per cent of the land area of the Community but accounted for 45 per cent of its population and about 60 per cent of its Gross Product. Inevitably, the question arises as to whether a far-reaching process of economic integration will lead to an acceleration of this concentration to the detriment of the relatively peripheral regions.[1] (Within the context of British membership of the EEC, the question can be put in the this form: 'Will Britain become the Northern Ireland of the Common Market?')

It is not difficult to recognize certain polarization factors at work. Thus some industries, in determining their location, will be

1. Peripheral areas do not always suffer. It is true that Sicily is more peripheral to the Rhine–Rhone axis than to Italy, but peripheral areas such as the Franco-German border positively gain from integration.

drawn towards a market, and this could imply a position close to the Rhine–Rhone axis. Then again the central axis creates external economies – for example, a skilled labour force and a disposition to accept the disciplines of industrial employment, not to mention the services of specialist commercial and financial institutions. It is easy to see the polarization factors at work but it is difficult to see any automatic balancing dispersal factor, except that full employment at the centre might eventually drive industry out into the peripheral regions. That is to say, the demand for labour might have an inflationary effect upon wage rates and earnings and land might become extremely scarce and expensive. However, the experience of the UK, with its growing concentration of industry in the Midlands and South East of England, gives little hope of any such automatic corrective tendency. The magnetic influence of the Paris region in France similarly suggests that a dispersal factor is not likely to rise spontaneously.

The nature of the Community regional problem

We turn now to the regional problem as it exists at the moment. Basically, and at the risk of some over-simplification, this resolves itself into two main kinds of problem. One is the under-development of regions which are primarily agricultural. The other relates to some of the older industrial areas where a contraction of activity in some staple industries has been and is taking place.

The classic under-development problem of the Community is the Italian Mezzogiorno. This is a region with a population of eighteen million (38 per cent of the Italian total) which comprises about half the land area of the country. The Mezzogiorno comprises the south (the regions of Abruzzi-Molise, Campania, Basilicata, Apulia and Calabria) together with the islands of Sicily and Sardinia. The 'southern problem' is best illustrated by statistics of income *per capita*. Within Italy itself there is a significant difference between the north and the south. Professor Saraceno (1965), estimated the *per capita* income in the south to be 50 per cent of the national average and 40 per cent of the northern region's. The contrast with the Community as a whole is of course even starker. Professor Levi Sandri, writing in the same year, but referring to 1958, stated that the *per capita* income of the most favoured region in the Community (Hamburg) was about seven times the corresponding figure for the least favoured Italian region (Calabria) (Levi Sandri, 1965).

Basically, the Mezzogiorno economy is founded on low-productivity subsistence agriculture. A considerable amount of effort and money has been devoted to industrialization. The Cassa per il Mezzogiorno (Development Fund for the South) has channelled vast sums into agricultural improvement and infrastructure investment and the state holding companies IRI and ENI have been obliged to channel at least 40 per cent of their investment into the south. In spite of all this the regional take-off into sustained industrial growth has not taken place in the Mezzogiorno. The rapidly growing population has had to find much of its opportunity through emigration to the north and the rest of the Community.

France provides the other example of persistent regional imbalances and major areas of under-development. The latter consist of central France (Massif Central), the south-west (Languedoc, Roussillon, Pyrénées and Aquitain), Brittany and Lower Normandy, Corsica and the Alpine region (Savoy). It should be noted that whereas the Italian south is heavily populated, all these French regions (except Brittany and Lower Normandy) are lightly populated. The migration of population from these areas has brought little benefit to the local economies. The farms remain under-capitalized and migration has indeed deprived these regions of the more energetic citizens who are indispensible if progress of any kind is to be made. By contrast the Paris region is prosperous. Its congestion and the resultant social costs are such that measures have been taken to arrest its growth in order to channel development to the less favoured regions. Much of this has been accomplished through the medium of the successive Plans.

The other main problem of the Community relates to the difficulties experienced in areas such as the Ruhr, the Sambre and Lorraine. These are areas which have been heavily industrialized for many years. Their prosperity was founded on iron ore reserves and coal, and the industries which were founded on these resources have begun to feel the effects of competition. The domestic iron ore industry has now got to meet the competition from cheap imported supplies. The domestic iron and steel industry has had to meet the competition from Japan and the newly industrialized countries. Coal of course faces the combined threat of oil and natural gas. Whether or not a severe regional problem develops depends on the rate of run-down of particular industries. In the Ruhr the relative efficiency of coal has meant a small decline which could easily be offset by the growth of other sectors. In the case of Belgian coal, however, where the pace of run-down has been rapid, severe regional problems have been encountered, as for example in the Borinage.

The role of Community institutions

Generally, when we wish to discover how the Community approaches problems in such fields as agriculture and industrial tariffs the natural response is to see what the Commission has said should be done and what the Council of Ministers has agreed to do. In the case of regional policy this is not true. The onus here lies mainly upon the national Governments. This does not mean that Community authorities play no role. In the first place the Commission has exercised an extremely important influence in drawing the attention of member-states to the regional problem and in sponsoring conferences on the subject. It has also addressed itself to specific problem areas. For example, in 1962 the Commission signed a contract with a Roman firm of planning consultants (Italconsult) to carry out studies for the promotion of an industrial development pole at Taranto-Bari in the heel of southern Italy. In 1965 the consultants produced a plan. Basically, this called for the establishment of a series of plants in various branches of the engineering industry. In addition it was proposed to establish ancillary industries simultaneously, to supply the needs of the engineering plants. The demands placed upon the ancillary industries had to be sufficient to enable the establishment of at least one plant of optimum size. The plan was really an attempt to create an industrial complex on the assumption that final producers would not set up unless there were component firms in existence to supply their needs, while at the same time component firms would not set up in business unless there were users of their products on the spot. The plan proposed to create 8000 jobs and required the investment of about £46 million.

Secondly, the Commission has a role to play in respect of state aids. The general aim of the Rome Treaty is to eliminate subsidies which distort the conditions of competition. However, under Article 92 of the Rome Treaty, exceptions may be made for aids which are

intended to promote the economic development of regions where the standard of living is abnormally low or where there exists serious under-employment ... [or which are] intended to facilitate the development of certain activities or of certain economic regions, provided that such aids do not change trading conditions to such a degree as would be contrary to the common interest.

The Commission does not have to permit such aids. For example, a regional aid might be more than necessary to overcome some locational disadvantage and might therefore be an indirect way of conferring an artificial competitive advantage. However, it must be said that little progress has been made in keeping a check on state regional aids. Indeed, if anything, the feature is one of retrogression. Clearly, when we speak about the need to keep a check on national policies we mean that it is important that aids should only be given where necessary and that, as between member-states, they should be harmonized. It makes no sense if one country schedules a particular type of problem as one which qualifies for aid, whilst another country does not view the problem in the same light, or does not give the same level of aid. There is a need, at the Community level, to identify the main types of regional problem, to devise means of measuring the degrees of severity of such problems and to reach an understanding about the levels of assistance which will be extended to problems of a particular severity. As yet no progress has been made in this field since the states in question refuse to agree upon any common levels of assistance. Moreover, there is some evidence which indicates that the member-states are now beginning to use regional aids in a competitive way to attract new industrial investment, particularly that emanating from the US. Not only is there a need for an attack upon the direct aid problem but it should also be borne in mind that there will still remain the problem of indirect aids arising out of generous infra-structure investment and low public-utility prices. This latter problem will be extremely difficult to deal with. The unwillingness to agree on common standards is another reflection of the desire of member-states to retain the power to attract foreign investment and to keep a hold of internally generated investment funds. It is therefore a manifestation of the same kind of problem as has been encountered in connexion with the European capital market.

Thirdly, Community institutions play a positive and important role in providing capital for the regions. One of these is the European Investment Bank which was established by the Rome Treaty. The Bank has a separate legal identity but it is required to work in the closest collaboration with the Governments of the member-states and the Commission. The originally authorized capital was one thousand million units of account, of which two hundred and fifty million was paid up by the Governments of the member-states. The capital as yet unpaid constitutes a guarantee for loans to be floated on capital markets. Originally it was intended that the Bank would endeavour to raise its capital by recourse to markets outside the Community. Unfortunately, due to a number of factors, one of which was the US adverse balance of payments and the restrictions placed on US citizens in subscribing to foreign loan issues, the Bank has had to turn to the Community capital markets for substantial help.

Article 30 of the Rome Treaty specifies three spheres of operation for the Bank. One is the financing of projects in the less developed regions. The second is the making of loans to enterprises that are forced to convert or modernize by virtue of the Common Market. Here the modernization or conversion has to arise as a result of tariff reductions and the like and the size and nature of the projects has to be such that they cannot be entirely financed by the member-states. The third sphere (which does not relate to the regional problem) concerns the financing of projects of common interest to member-states. Again the project has to be beyond the means of individual member-states if it is to qualify for assistance.

The Bank in making loans does not finance the whole of the project. Rather it finds the last increment of finance necessary to get the project off the ground when all other sources of funds have been exhausted. This means that the amount it has lent severely under-estimates its impact and importance. In 1966 the Bank's average participation in projects was 22 per cent. During the first ten years of its existence, from 1 January to 31 December 1967, the Bank lent nine hundred and seventy-eight million units of account.

Not all the loans of the Bank have gone to the member-states. During the first ten years of its operations member-states received 77 per cent of loans by value. Associated states benefitted from the balance. Within the Community Italy has been the main beneficiary. A total of 40 per cent of the loans have gone into industrial investment and 60 per cent into infrastructure.

In discussing the role of Community institutions we should not neglect the Agricultural Guidance and Guarantee Fund. As was indicated in chapter 5, part of its function is to assist in the financing of structural improvements in agriculture. Since some of the most acute regional problems are associated with low-productivity agriculture the Fund clearly has a vital role to play. In some areas agriculture is over-manned. This arises not only from the small size of firms but also from fragmentation. The formation of larger consolidated farms would reduce the amount of labour required per acre. Provided the surplus labour could be siphoned off the land, those left in agriculture could enjoy higher incomes. As a complement to the activities of the Fund it will therefore be necessary to create new employment opportunities in industry and services.

It should also be mentioned that the present Commission disposes of the power (originally given to the High Authority of the ECSC) to make finance available to develop new sources of employment in areas where the products covered by the Paris Treaty have been declining. This is referred to as Redevelopment Policy.

Social Policy

There are four strands to Community social policy. The first is really contained in Article 2 of the Rome Treaty which lays down the tasks which the Community has to achieve. These are said to be the promotion of

... an harmonious development of economic activities, a continuous and balanced expansion, an increase in stability, an accelerated raising of the standard of living ....

As Kitzinger (1961) has pointed out, the main preoccupation of the EEC is with the enlargement of the Community cake. Such an enlargement has social as well as economic implications. The question of the distribution of the cake, and in particular the question of the level of social services and the like, is largely left to the member-states in the first instance. In the longer term the influence of harmonization may be felt; this is discussed below.

The second strand of social policy relates to labour mobility. As we have already noted, under the Rome Treaty social policy is not confined to those spheres of activity which involve financial hand-outs. It also covers those policies which enable people to better themselves by virtue of the removal of restrictions on their freedom. The establishment of conditions in which a worker can move from one member-state to another without loss of social service benefits and so forth, are acts of social policy. In a significant number of individual cases such opportunities almost certainly provide a more powerful means of social improvement than mere doles to the unemployed. The subject of freedom of movement of labour has, however, been dealt with in chapter 4 and we shall not discuss it further here.

The third strand relates to social security harmonization and closely related issues, such as equal pay for equal work. The harmonization issue was a feature of the negotiations leading up to the Paris and Rome Treaties. It should perhaps be stressed at this point that in the Six, as compared with the UK (and Scandinavia), the employer contributes a much higher proportion of social security revenue. Thus in 1962 French employers contributed 69 per cent whereas the state contributed 7 per cent and the insured 20 per cent. This contrasts with the U K where the figures were 21 per cent, 52 per cent and 27 per cent respectively. Because of the fact that within the Six the burden on French employers was particularly severe the French Government attempted, at the time when the Paris Treaty was being negotiated, to include provisions for the immediate harmonization of social costs of production. In practice the High Authority was not given the power to harmonize social conditions and Article 3 merely refers to the general intention to harmonize conditions in an upward direction. In negotiations leading up to the Rome Treaty the issue was again raised by the French. They argued that the higher rate of social security payments – very approximately 50 per cent on top wages – raised their costs of production and placed them in a competitively vulnerable position. They also cited other examples of exceptional burdens, such as the law on equal pay for equal work and paid-holiday schemes. Once again the French did not succeed in obtaining an explicit agreement and powers to harmonize social security burdens within a given time-span. Article 117 states that the member-states agree on the need to promote better conditions of living, work and employment so as to lead to their progressive harmonization and improvement. The Article also enunciates the belief that the operation of the Common Market will favour the harmonization of social systems. The Community position may be said to be that harmonization in an upward direction is desirable. In order to achieve the objectives of Article 117, Article 118 lays upon the Commission the task of promoting close collaboration between the member-states in a number of fields including employment, labour law and working conditions, basic and advanced vocational training, social security, protection against occupational accidents and diseases, occupational hygiene, the law of trade unions and collective bargaining between employers and workers.

On the face of it, it cannot be said that a great deal has been achieved so far by way of harmonization. The Commission has sought to stimulate the interest of the member-states in comparative social security standards. For example, in 1962 it sponsored a conference on this subject. But the ability of the Commission to secure concrete results is limited. While states cannot refuse to collaborate in studies of particular problems, they retain the power to accept or reject the results. States are also prone to guard their independence jealously, as the following indicates:

It would be foolish to deny that the full unfolding of the possibilities contained in the functions of the Commission would lead it deep into the social affairs of the member-states and it can fairly claim a general mandate for its interest in the action taken by states in the social field, for its attempt to encourage inter-state co-operation and for the strengthening of a sense of European concern. States, on the other hand, tend to resist action by the Commission which seems to fall outside the specific mandate of the Treaty. Under such circumstances it would clearly be impracticable for the Commission to attempt to impose changes and to try to insist upon unifying national laws or practices. For the time being, it is a sufficient aim to work for a reasonable harmony in different social systems, so that individuals, in similar circumstances, have comparable rights and benefits wherever they may live. To work for a situation in which, to take a few examples, social security cover is comparable, hours of work, length of holidays and working conditions broadly equivalent, is a more modest but more immediately realisable aim which does not necessitate complete structural uniformity (Collins, 1966, pp. 42–3).

The achievement of harmonization is, however, likely to be a long-drawn-out process.

It is perhaps worth mentioning at this point that in this sphere, and indeed in others, it would be a mistake to see progress to harmonization as depending merely upon Council directives on common or minimum standards. With increasing integration market forces may bring about greater uniformity. Then again, closer contact of the kind provided by Community institutions as well as the publicity given to the Commission studies of relative standards, may stimulate the spirit of emulation.

Some theoretical consideration has been given to the subject of the necessity for harmonization of social costs of production. By and large the conclusion seems to be that the matter is something of a red herring. Balassa's conclusions are that, except for special cases,

... the harmonization of entrepreneur-financed social programs is not necessary for the proper functioning of a union, and measures of harmonization, if undertaken, are likely to cause distortions in the pattern of production and trade and will give rise to undesirable factor movements, no matter whether the social charges are of general or special incidence (Balassa, 1962).

Although the matter is of some complexity the following points are worth making.

Economic analysis would not suggest that wages should be harmonized within an economic union. Is there then a case for harmonizing the costs of social benefits borne by entrepreneurs? The general answer seems to be in the negative. This view, which appears to have commended itself to the authors of the Ohlin Report (International Labour Office, 1956), is based on the argument that social payments borne by entrepreneurs are ultimately shifted to wage earners. Wages in countries were social charges have risen most have increased less than wages in countries where social charges have risen least. Another way of putting it is to say that where entrepreneurs have had to pay high payroll taxes (to finance social security) they have been constrained to offer lower wages and vice-versa. There is indeed some empirical evidence which points in this direction.

Theoretically speaking, we can ask how the shifting can occur. The process depends on the assumptions made. Let us assume that there is perfect price and wage flexibility and that wage earners regard social benefits as part of their earnings. If social benefits rise then both the supply and demand schedules for labour would shift in such a way that the wage rate would fall by an amount which reflected the rise in social benefits – employment would remain unchanged. Suppose, however, that there is a downward rigidity of wages and prices. The course of events would be different but it could be argued that the shifting would substantially and progressively occur. As productivity increased, entrepreneurs would concede wage increases which were less than they would have been in the absence of the rise in social benefits.

A few general conclusions can be drawn. Firstly, let us consider the case of social-security charges borne uniformly by all industries. If the social charges imposed in the past have been absorbed into the cost structure of individual member-states (in the way we discussed above) then it should be pointed out that harmonization of social charges will cause difficulties. Thus if a member-state had experienced a relatively small rise in social charges then wages would have tended to rise all the more as a result. On the other hand, in other member-states the reverse situation may have applied. Other things being equal, the latter states would have a cost structure in which social-security costs constituted a larger percentage than in the former state. If harmonization took place on the basis of the latter state-security level (or an average of the two), the price of exports of the former state would rise and deflation or realignment of exchange rates would have to occur. Secondly, let us relax the assumption of a uniform level of social-security charges. Suppose the incidence in a member-state varied. Would this lead to distortions? The answer appears to be in the negative. So long as the social-security burden can be shifted by entrepreneurs to wage earners then all that would happen would be that the composition of labour costs (the proportionate importance of social-security charges and wages) would differ from industry to industry. Similar reasoning leads to the conclusion that no difficulties arise if there are inter-country differences in the social-security charges levied on particular industries. Thirdly, it can also be argued that harmonization is not necessary as between member-states in order to prevent undesirable movements of capital and labour. Indeed, Balassa argues that due to the influence of price and wage rigidities harmonization could lead to perverse movements of capital and labour.

With regard to the question of equal pay for equal work it should be noted that the French secured what they no doubt regarded as a success. Article 119 of the Rome Treaty required that during the first stage each member-state would introduce the equal pay for equal work system. In practice the implementation of this Article was at first left to member-states and not surprisingly some dragged their feet. As a result the implementation fell behind the timetable prescribed by the Treaty. The Commission therefore stepped in and consequently the states accepted a resolution to the effect that differences were to be eliminated by the end of 1964. According to one commentator writing in 1966:

Progress so far has been mixed. In those countries where wages are fixed for many people by collective agreements, it seems that women's wages are being progressively harmonized with those of men although not always as quickly as the Resolution anticipated. Examples of more subtle disabilities resulting from the regrading of jobs and the depressing of women into low-grade work are, however, still reported. It is clearly arguable how much power the Commission holds. Much must be left to employers and to union organizations to watch over the application of the principle 'on the ground' and to make information available about the extent of its fulfilment. The Commission can clearly encourage this work and give particular support to the women's organizations, but where women are unorganized and their wages inadequately protected the Commission can do little except encourage the appropriate Government to take action (Collins, 1966, p. 38).

The reason why the French pressed the equal pay for equal work point is obvious enough. In industries where the wages of women were raised above the level they normally would have been in the absence of the law governing equal pay, French industry would be at a competitive disadvantage in relation to member-states which did not have such a law. The general espousal of equal pay under the Treaty therefore amounted to agreeing to the proposition that equalization would remedy distortions which would otherwise be caused by different legal provisions. It should, however, be pointed out that equal pay is a social and not an economic principle. Even if equal productivity is forthcoming this does not justify equal pay. According to conventional wage theory the productivity of workers relates only to the demand side of the labour market. An entrepreneur will be prepared to take on a different quantity of labour at each wage rate, the actual amount being determined by the rule that the marginal revenue product of labour should be equal to the wage rate. Given equal productivity of male and female operatives an entrepreneur would be indifferent as between the two. However, on the supply side at each and every wage rate the amount of female labour offering itself might be significantly different from the amount of male labour on offer. The absolute equalization of wages paid to males and females could therefore give rise to the unemployment of female labour. This loss would have to be set against the elimination of distortions discussed above.

The fourth strand of Community social policy is connected with the European Social Fund which plays much the same role under the Rome Treaty that Readaptation Policy played and still plays under the Paris Treaty. The Social Fund has as its main object the establishment of a high degree of geographical and occupational mobility among workers within the Community. The broad lines within which the Fund operates are laid down in Articles 123 to 128 of the Treaty. The main form of its operation is that the Fund reimburses Governments with 50 per cent of any expenditure which they incur in retraining or resettling unemployed or under-employed labour, or in supporting the wages of labour which has temporarily been laid off during the conversion of an enterprise to other lines of production. In a sense, therefore, although we have chosen to treat the Fund under social policy it does in fact provide a method of dealing with the regional unemployment problem.

The retraining grants are only repayable when retraining is the only way of bringing workers back into employment, and such grants are only paid when the worker has been employed for at least six months in this new occupation. Resettlement allowances are only paid when the workers concerned have been obliged to change their place of residence, and again such grants are only paid six months after employment in a new position. Reconversion support (to maintain gross wages at 90 per cent of the former level) is only given to schemes which have been submitted to the Commission by the state concerned and have been given the approval of the latter prior to introduction. To qualify for assistance a reconversion need not have arisen because of the effect of the new forces unleashed by the Common Market. In practice no scheme of reconversion has qualified for assistance from the Fund so far.

The initiative for using the Fund lies with member-states. The Fund does not have a budget limit. It is supplied with funds by the member-states in whatever amount is required to pay the requests for 50 per cent assistance. Under the Rome Treaty a scale of contributions has been fixed which deviates from the contributions to the general Community budget most noticeably in respect of Italy. The latter pays only 20 per cent to the Social Fund whereas its contribution to the Community budget is 28 per cent. It is therefore apparent that the intention of the Fund was to help Italy, and in practice this appears to have been the effect. During the period up to and including 1965 there was a net transfer of $4·7 million to Italy and the Netherlands (the latter's share was very small) from other member-states, especially West Germany.

During the period September 1960 to December 1967 assistance under the Social Fund amounted to just over $54 million. The number of persons benefiting was 553,000. The general trend is for the number of workers retrained and resettled under the Fund to fall. On the other hand expenditure from the Fund in 1967 was the highest in its history – $13,849,037 in respect of 47,586 workers retrained and resettled. The sharp rise in 1967 was due to a general rise in retraining costs – in some member-states allowances and concessions for workers during training were increased substantially.

It has been increasingly recognized that the sphere of operations of the Fund is somewhat narrow and needs to be redefined in the light of the problems currently confronting the Community. In 1965 the Commission submitted proposals to increase the effectiveness of the Fund although as yet the Council of Ministers has not finally pronounced on the matter. The Commission proposes that the Fund should be used to help the vocational training not only of unemployed or under-employed workers but also of employed workers whose jobs are threatened because they lack qualifications or because they are no longer adequately equipped for modern production techniques. The Fund should also help to maintain the wages of workers who have lost their jobs through the closing of their firms in regions suffering from or threatened with unemployment and who are waiting to be re-employed by new enterprises setting up in the region. Also the Fund should participate in the building of training centres in those regions which were not particularly well equipped in this respect. Finally, it should help to provide low-cost housing for migrant workers and their families and also to assist with social services in respect of such workers.

As already indicated, under the Paris Treaty the Commission is empowered to grant non-repayable readaptation assistance in the form of compensation to tide workers over until they are able to find new employment, resettlement allowances and technical retraining grants. Between March 1954 and December 1967 about 331,000 workers received just over $100 million by way of re-adaptation assistance.

7 Macro-Economic, Medium-Term and Industrial Policy

Macro-Economic Policy
The fact of interdependence

The need for a macro-economic policy at the Community level springs basically from the fact that economic integration implies that each national economy becomes increasingly dependent on the others. This increased interdependence and sensitivity requires that there be some co-ordination and rules governing the way in which member-states control their levels of activity, and in particular the way in which they deal with balance-of-payments problems.

The origins of the increased interdependence are not difficult to demonstrate. If an economy inflates its spending then some of it spills over on to the other member-states. The spill-over takes the form of imports from the member-states. The other member-states therefore become more prosperous and in turn spend money on goods produced by the state which originally inflated. Such an inter-action is likely where there are no tariffs and other barriers inhibiting the flow of spending between states. When, on the other hand, there is substantial tariff protection, an increase in internally generated demand may merely drive up the internal price level, since imported supplies may be rendered uncompetitive by the tariff and will therefore not enter to absorb the extra demand. (There is of course a limit to this argument. When the internal price level has risen sufficiently to render imports, with duty added, competitive, the spill-over via imports will occur.)

In the absence of tariff protection the effect which an inflation of demand in one country has on the economies of other member-states will of course have a limit. Such an inflation will, as we have already seen, increase imports and will probably reduce the quantity of goods available for export. Other things being equal, a balance-of-payments problem will force the government to bring the inflation under control. A deflation of internal demand will have a contrary effect on the economies of other member-states. The deflating state will import less and the other states will be less prosperous. The latter will then import less from the deflating state.

The increased interdependence is made manifest in other ways. Anti-slump policies become less effective and more costly. For example, if a Government embarked on a public works policy to boost domestic employment, some of the spending would find its way abroad and would therefore create employment elsewhere. Therefore, where an economy is open to trade, more would have to be spent to achieve a given increase in employment than would be the case in an economy closed to trade. The greater cost can be measured in two ways. One is the cost of the public works programme. The other is the foreign exchange cost arising from imports.

Control of the economy is also affected in other ways. For example, a rise in interest rates designed to check spending in times of boom can be frustrated by virtue of the fact that borrowers can resort to the capital and credit markets of other member-states in order to obtain finance at cheaper rates. If monetary policy consists of making credit less easily available then again it can be frustrated by access to finance from abroad. Exchange rates are an obviously sensitive area. A unilateral change, for example a devaluation, could disturb the balance between close trading partners. Also, when capital is free to move between states uncertainty about the future level of exchange rates can lead to massive speculative movements. These can be very upsetting as was the case as between France and Germany in 1968 and 1969.

The rules

The Community rules for dealing with cyclical and balance-of-payments problems are contained in Articles 103 to 109. Article 103 is the only one relating to cyclical policy. It states that member-states shall regard as a matter of common concern their short-term economic policies and shall consult with each other and the Commission on measures to be taken in response to current circumstances. Article 104 enjoins each member-state to walk the all too familiar tight-rope: they shall pursue the economic policies necessary to maintain equilibrium of the balance of payments and confidence in the currency whilst simultaneously ensuring high employment and stability of prices. In order to achieve all this, Article 105 requires the member-states to co-ordinate their economic policies. This Article specifically calls for co-ordination in monetary matters as well as collaboration between budgetary authorities and central banks. Article 106 need not detain us – it is designed to deal with the problem of exchange control inhibiting the integration of commodity and capital markets. Article 107 requires each member-state to treat its policy with regard to exchange rates as a matter of common interest. This Article also provides remedies against changes in exchange rates which are incompatible with the Rome Treaty. Article 108 states that where a state is already experiencing, or is threatened by, balance-of-payments difficulties, the Commission shall investigate the measures which the state has taken or intends to take and shall make recommendations. This Article also provides for mutual financial assistance, either by means of a concerted approach to international institutions (this obviously refers to the IMF), or directly by the Community. Article 109 was discussed earlier in connexion with the free movement of capital. It enables a member-state to take immediate protective measures if a sudden balance-of-payments crisis arises. However, any state taking such emergency action has to reckon with the fact that the Council may subsequently, after the Commission has given its opinion and the Monetary Committee has been consulted, suspend such protective measures.

Policy in practice

It is apparent that Articles 103 and 105 both call for close collaboration and co-ordination in those fields which influence national levels of activity and therefore trade between member-states. In order to enable this co-ordination to occur the Community has created a number of committees. One of the most important is the Monetary Committee consisting of two members from each state and two from the Commission. The Committee was expressly called for by the Rome Treaty and came into existence in 1958.

It meets in Brussels ten or twelve times a year. Sessions are devoted to a general examination of the overall economic and monetary situation and also to a general study of the situation in one member-state, the formula being that of a 'cross-examination' by the representatives of another member country and of the Commission. The Committee has formulated frequent opinions, which are confidential, to the Commission and the Council. In 1964 the Council formally extended the functions of the Committee to include the co-ordination of the positions of the member-states in the framework of international monetary bodies, where the Community has in recent years been in a strong position resulting from its sound monetary situation (Palmer *et al.*, 1968, pp. 223–4).

In 1960 the Council of Ministers brought into existence the Committee on Short-Term Economic Trends – again this is drawn from member-states and the Commission. The governors of the five central banks (Luxembourg does not have a separate central bank) meet regularly, not only at the monthly meetings at the Bank of International Settlements but also, since April 1964, in the Community's own Committee of Central Bank Governors. This Committee, apart from concerning itself with internal Common Market affairs, has also played an important and influential external role, as for example in the case of policy formulation concerning the size of credits to be granted to the UK and the acceptable degree of devaluation by the latter in November 1967. The year 1964 also saw the creation of the Medium-Term Economic Policy Committee – more will be said about this in the next section. In 1965 the Budgetary Committee was established which brings together senior officials of national ministries of economic affairs in an attempt to co-ordinate national budgets.

The Commission, of course, exercises a watching brief over the course of events within the national economies and encourages policies which take account of the interdependence of the various economies. Apart from bringing its views to bear in the various committees, quarterly reports are produced on the situation and outlook for the economies of each member-state and the Community as a whole. Although these reports are prepared in collaboration with national civil services, they reflect the judgement of the Commission. Also, at the January session of the European

Parliament it is traditional for the member of the Commission responsible for economic and financial affairs (previously M. Robert Marjolin and now M. Raymond Barre) to present the Commission's assessment of the economic situation and the prospects to come.

The various committees just mentioned and the Commission exercise an important influence via the Recommendations adopted by the Council of Ministers. For example, in 1964 when the Community generally was facing a strong inflationary threat proposals concerning national economic policy were submitted by the Commission to the Short-Term and Monetary Committees and were adopted by the Council. The Recommendation included a limit to the annual growth of public expenditure by 5 per cent, a requirement to finance any unavoidable spending above this ceiling by taxation, a call for the maintenance and tightening up of existing credit policy and for the introduction of a productivity-based incomes policy.

Despite institutional developments the Commission has been dissatisfied with the effectiveness of co-ordination particularly as this becomes more important as the states have become progressively more open to each other. In December 1968 the Commission addressed a memorandum, *The Coordination of Economic Policy and Monetary Cooperation within the Community*, to the Council of Ministers. This called for more effective consultation on short and medium-term national policies. The Commission also submitted a draft directive which sought to introduce compulsory consultation before the taking of any national decision, relating to the trend of prices, incomes and employment, overall budgetary policy and tax policy, which affected the economies of other member-states. In January 1970 the Council of Finance and Economics Ministers established the machinery for prior consultation on short-term policy measures.

The idea that exchange rates are of common interest is something of an understatement of the views which have recently prevailed, at least within the Commission. Its view is that the Community must continue to adopt fixed as opposed to flexible exchange rates and to maintain the existing parities. It will be remembered in discussing the free movement of capital that the

Segré Report favoured even the abolition of the small margin of fluctuation around the official parity. The justification for not disturbing the existing parities is based on two arguments. The first, a traditional argument, is that varying rates are a hindrance to commercial activity. The second is connected with the common agricultural policy. As we have already seen, the prices of agricultural products are fixed in terms of the Community's unit of account whose gold content is equal to that of the US Dollar. If a member-state revalues its currency this implies a fall in the price of food to farmers in terms of the domestic currency, whilst a devaluation raises prices. Such a change in prices would therefore inevitably interfere with the arrangements made under the common agricultural policy.

The view that exchange rates must be fixed and stay put has been re-emphasized recently by M. Raymond Barre. In his view neither the crawling peg, nor wider bands of fluctuation for existing exchange rates, are acceptable within the EEC framework. In this connexion it should be noted that in February 1968 the Commission submitted a memorandum to the finance ministers of the Six to the effect that studies should be carried out by the Committee of Central Bank Governors and the Monetary Committee on two issues. The first related to the possibility of member-states committing themselves not to change exchange rate parities except by joint agreement.[1] The second concerned the possibility that fluctuations in exchange rates as between member-states should be totally eliminated and that identical spreads should be agreed *vis-à-vis* non-member states. All this does not of course imply that there is a uniformity of view within the Community on this matter. For example, recently Guido Carli, the governor of the Bank of Italy, in a report to the Monnet Action Committee for the United States of Europe, advocated the general applicability of the crawling-peg system. Under this arrangement quarterly or even monthly adjustments up and down would be possible up to a maximum of 2 per cent per annum. However, there can be no doubt that the official Community

1. Assuming British membership of the EEC, and given the British propensity to inflate, fixed exchange rates could be more costly than the Common Agricultural Policy.

view is that exchange rates must be fixed and devaluations and revaluations must be ruled out. This became clear in February 1970 when the Council of Ministers outlined the policies to be adopted in order to attain economic and monetary union by 1978–80. High on the list of priorities was fixity of exchange rates.

The French devaluation of August 1969 of course came as a rude shock to the Community. All the more so as it was apparently undertaken without consultation. This episode does moreover call into question the notion that exchange parities should remain undisturbed. While ever the control of monetary and fiscal weapons lies in the hands of member-state Governments it is quite probable that national price levels will not move in parallel and as a result exchange rates which once were right will sooner or later cease to be right. Indeed exchange rates can cease to be right quite quickly when individual systems are subjected to the kind of shocks which occurred in France in and after May 1968. In short, a system of fixed and unchanging exchange rates, which admittedly paves the way towards a common European currency, is only likely to work when monetary and fiscal policies are centrally controlled within some federal system. It is of course apparent that the Community is a long way from such a goal. In such a system macro-economic policy would be concerned with the overall position in the Community and the levels of activity in member-states would be akin to the regional problems at present experienced at national level.

The benefits of a flexible exchange-rates system are reinforced by the tendency for politicians to regard the maintenance of the rate as a matter of national pride. The reluctance in 1968 and 1969 of France to devalue and Germany to revalue are examples of this.

As has already been pointed out, Article 108 states that when states are involved in or threatened by balance-of-payments crisis the Commission shall investigate the measures proposed or undertaken and make recommendations. Apparently Article 108 has never been formally invoked but in 1964 when Italy faced a severe balance-of-payments problem the Commission acted in accordance with the first paragraph. It investigated the situation and measures taken and advised the Italian Government on the approach which should be adopted. More recently the Commission has sought to put some flesh on the bones of Article 108 by proposing in the December 1968 memorandum a system of mutual financial assistance in time of crisis. This was acted upon by the Common Market Ministers of Finance and Economics in July 1969 when they asked the central banks to work out a reciprocal drawing-rights scheme under which short-term aid would be made available for member-states in balance-of-payments difficulties. In January 1970 the Council of Finance and Economics Ministers formally authorized the Central Banks to establish the monetary aid scheme. This provides for monetary assistance up to $2000 million. Each member-state can automatically draw up to the quota of their contribution to the first $1000 million. The quotas are $300 million for France and West Germany, $200 million for Italy and $100 million each for the Netherlands and Belgium/Luxembourg. Such aid is of three months' duration. The second $1000 million can be made available for three months, and renewed for a further three, and in principle any state could draw the whole amount provided the other states had made no call upon it.

Medium-Term Policy

The origins of this policy lie in the Action Programme for the Second Stage which the Commission produced in 1962. This document was the Commission's chart for progress following the successful completion of the first stage of the transition period. This memorandum, which immediately achieved something of the status of a *cause célèbre* by being the occasion of a heated debate in the European Parliament, seemed to some to exhibit a kind of economic schizophrenia. Not only did it repeat what was already down to be the Community's philosophy in respect of competition policy, but it introduced – under the name of programming – what some took to be contrary proposals which, if they did not constitute central planning, at least appeared to contain a threat to the free-market system. The most sensitive critics were the West Germans of the Neo-Liberal school. Dr Ludwig Erhard also found the proposals at variance with his concept of the social-market economy and strongly criticized the Commission's proposals in the European Parliament.

The word 'programming' is conceptually capable of being defined in a number of ways. It can be a device for co-ordinating the various economic policies of Governments. Given that Governments tend to intervene in the workings of the economy, programming can give coherence and direction to such interventions in the light of forecasts of development. Equally well, programming can be a technique for influencing the decisions of the private sector. Here there is a spectrum of possibilities. Firstly, the Government can produce long-term projections which constitute non-binding lines of guidance. Secondly, a distinction can be made between mere projections and official targets. The latter are likely to be more influential for two reasons. One is that the Government is in some sense committed to a target and can therefore use such instruments as it commands to enable that target to be reached. The second is that the private sector will assume that the target is feasible because it is part of an overall plan in which the resources required for the target growth in the industry in question are consistent with other demands upon resources. Thirdly, the Government may seek to bring its influence to bear in order to guarantee the realization of targets. This can be done, as was the case in French indicative planning, by involving industry in the formulation of targets. It can be argued that being involved in drawing up the plan tends to generate a willingness to co-operate in making its fulfillment possible. Also, participation by industry in formulating targets engenders the view that the drawing up of a programme is an exercise in coherence; that is to say, the growth targets of individual industries are consistent one with another. This inculcates the idea that if everyone plays his agreed role the plan will succeed. This was the philosophy behind French planning. However, it was buttressed by another important factor, namely that the Government disposed of a whole range of inducements such as tax abatements, export subsidies, privileged access to credit, specially low interest rates, investment grants for regional development and subsidies for research. These could and were used to induce action consistent with the plan. Finally, programming or planning can of course take the Soviet pattern. Here mutually consistent targets are drawn up in physical terms and the state disposes of the power to direct resources in order to fulfill the plan. Needless to say, such a system precludes private ownership as the means of production and the profit motive in the normally accepted Western sense.

On the face of it the furore, particularly in West German circles, was misplaced. Planning at the Community level in the sense of influencing the private sector on the French model (the Soviet system was clearly not even a starter) was impossible in that the Treaty of Rome did not provide the Community organs with the necessary powers. In practice the Commission's objective in proposing the introduction of a Community programme was really the co-ordination of the policies of authorities, as opposed to directing the production and investment decisions of the private sector. The Commission's adoption of programming was based on a number of factors. One was that the Rome Treaty required the Community authorities to ensure the co-ordination of the economic policies of the member-states in the field of cyclical, monetary and balance-of-payments policy. The other was the Treaty's call for common policies in agriculture, transport and energy. Clearly these have to be guided by a general view of the progressive development of the Community economy as a whole. (It is, however, only fair to point out that West German reactions were not without some justification. The statements in the Action Programme on the nature and objectives of Community programming were somewhat obscure and the phraseology left open the possibility that some kind of influence on particular industries, perhaps by industrial targets, would be operative.) However, there were other forces at work which pointed to the need for a Community programming system. At the national level forces were operating which were rendering French national planning less effective whilst internal developments in West Germany were rendering opinion there more favourable to the idea of some form of programming both at national and Community level.

French support for the Community programme derived in considerable measure from the fact that the unfolding of the Common Market was rendering national planning increasingly impossible. The increased openness of the French system meant that it was more difficult to forecast the future development of the economy in aggregate or by sectors and industries. Equally, it was more difficult to control the economy since what happened to French industry depended on events in other member-states. Difficulties caused by the free movement of goods were complemented by the free movement of factors such as capital. Then again, under the common agricultural policy control of French agriculture ceased to be a national prerogative. Finally, many of the state aids which the Government employed to induce compliance with the plan were found to conflict with the Rome Treaty.

The medium-term policy would not, however, have come to fruition if there had not been a change of heart on the part of West Germany. A number of factors led to the change of direction. One of the most important was the rapid growth of public investment and public spending generally. This required the drawing up of medium- or longer-term programmes of public finance. These in turn had to be related to forecasts of the growth of other sectors of the economy. In July 1963 the Commission addressed a Recommendation to the Council of Ministers on medium-term policy and in April 1964 the Council of Ministers decided to form a Medium-Term Policy Committee. This consisted of two members (and two alternates) from each member-state together with representatives from the Commission. Its task was to prepare a preliminary draft programme of medium-term economic policy. This in turn required the production of projections of economic growth. The latter function was placed in the hands of a separate Groupe d'Étude des Perspectives Économiques à Moyen Terme. This group was made up of independent experts working for the Commission. Thus, those producing the forecasts were to be separate from those erecting the policy programme on the basis of them. The resulting programme, which would deal with the economic policies necessary to keep economies on the course mapped out for them, would then be submitted to the Council of Ministers and by agreeing to it the member-states would be expressing an intention to act in accordance with it. The first programme passed through all these stages and was finally adopted by the Council in February 1967.

The projections for the whole Community were that Gross

Domestic Product would grow at 4·3 per cent per annum between 1966 and 1970. This compared with a growth of 4·9 per cent in the previous five years. In order to achieve this target, productive investment would have to increase at 6·1 per cent per annum and public investment at 8·5 per cent. In order for the latter to be achieved private consumption would have to be constrained; a growth rate of 4·1 per cent was proposed.

Three points are worth emphasizing. One is that disaggregation has been avoided. Although the Commission is in favour of breaking down global projections, German opposition to providing projections for particular industries is very strong. The second point is that both the policy and the projections are to be reviewed annually. Finally, although programming was a new development within the EEC it was of long standing in the ECSC. For many years the High Authority drew up 'general objectives' for coal and steel. These were medium-term forecasts of the likely evolution of demand. The High Authority required that it be notified of investments above a minimum size and issued reasoned opinions on them in the light of forecasts of demand. Unfavourable opinions were intended to make the raising of outside finance difficult whilst the High Authority itself would obviously refuse to give financial assistance to projects which did not fit in with the general objectives of growth.

Industrial Policy

In recent years a number of problems have dominated discussions of economic policy within the EEC. These have included the implications of British membership, the shape and financing of the common agricultural policy, and last, but not least, the question of concentration and competition in Community industry. The latter problem has resolved itself into two main issues. On the one hand, there has been strong pressure within the EEC to evolve policies at Community and national level which would hasten the process of concentration, and therefore the emergence of larger firms which could compete with the giant enterprises of the US. On the other hand, there has also been a recognition of the fact that the Community needs a policy which can effectively deal with concentrations of economic power. Thus, while both these viewpoints have been concerned with concentration and competition, the former has envisaged concentration as a means of bringing about more equal conditions of competition with US enterprises, whether located in the US, or within the Community itself, whereas the latter viewpoint has focused attention on the need to preserve competition within the Community.

The strongest support for increased concentration has come from industry, specifically from UNICE (Union des Industries de la Communauté Européenne), the Patronat Français, and also from the French Government. The Commission, on the other hand, whilst not denying the need for viable enterprises within the Community, has taken the view that policy should seek to create conditions which would guarantee that the factors affecting concentration (such as taxation and company law) would be neutral in their effects. That is to say, they should neither artificially stimulate nor artificially impede the concentration process. Then again, it has been recognized that the existing anti-trust powers of the Rome Treaty do not really empower the Brussels Commission to prevent undesirable concentrations from taking place and that an amplification of powers in this field is therefore called for.

The drive for greater concentration

When businessmen in the Six contemplate the structure of their industry, their overwhelming preoccupation has been with the contrast between the size of firms there and in the UK, Japan, and above all the US. Community industrialists have seen the size contrast as meaning that they would be at a disadvantage in the competitive struggle for third country markets, whilst, on the other hand, the Kennedy Round and the setting up of American subsidiaries within the Six have meant that the domestic market cannot be taken for granted.

Two main questions arise here in connexion with this argument, for greater concentration. First, is the size contrast valid? Second, if it is, what are the advantages of size and are there any limits to them?

The evidence available, which is far from perfect, shows that in respect of plant size the US has an advantage over at least some of the Common Market countries. One way of demonstrating the size difference is to measure the size of plant by the number employed. If plants are divided into those which employ 1–49 workers, 50–99, 100–499, 500–999, and 1000 and above then the general picture is clear. The US has a smaller proportion of its employees engaged in plants of the smaller categories, and a notably larger proportion in the 1000-plus category. However, in the middle ranges there is no great contrast. The average size of plant in the Six as a whole is somewhat smaller than that in the US, and this is most clearly so in the case of France, Italy and Belgium. Average plant size in West Germany, on the other hand, appears to be broadly comparable with that in the US.

Data concerning the steel industry of the ECSC – an industry in which substantial economies of large scale production do exist – indicate that the size of steel plants in the Six is well below that of Japan and the US. For example, in 1965 only 7·4 per cent of ECSC crude steel production came from plants of over six million metric tons annual capacity as against 81 per cent in the US and 49 per cent in Japan. On the other hand, 39 per cent of production in the ECSC came from plants of less than two million tons annual capacity, whereas in the US and Japan the figures were 15 per cent and 6 per cent respectively.

So far we have been looking at the situation in respect of plant size. However, it is the contrast in the size of firms which has been a major plank in the argument of those who seek to achieve greater concentration within the Community. Readers will be familiar with the figures of turnover which have appeared in the magazine *Fortune*. These were seized upon by UNICE, and the contrast between the turnover of the three biggest Community enterprises and the three biggest US enterprises in particular industries has been repeatedly stressed. This exercise has been carried out with respect to the automboile, chemical, rubber, electrical, steel and petroleum industries for the year 1963. Two conclusions emerge from this type of analysis. The first is that calculations of the ratio of the size of the biggest Community firm to its opposite number in the US show that in two-thirds of the cases the former is less than half the size of the latter. Indeed, for the first four of the six industries just listed, even the third American enterprise is considerably larger than the largest Community firm. Second, within the Community itself it is clear that the majority of the largest firms are West German, with France coming second but trailing well behind. It is the discrepancy between the size of firms within the Community and the US, and the particularly poor position of the French, that has been at the root of European, and particularly French, fears about competition.

So much for the data that have been used in justification of the proposal for greater concentraton within the European Community. However, sheer size cannot in itself be a very persuasive argument for adopting a policy of greater concentration. It needs to be demonstrated that the greater size of US enterprises carries with it certain advantages. Conventionally, the advantages of size resolve themselves into two kinds – the economies of large-scale production and distribution, and the capacity to carry out R and D, which requires relatively large amounts of finance that only the larger enterprises can dispose of.

Generally speaking, there are available to firms in manufacturing industry economies of large-scale production and distribution which make it possible for them by becoming larger to lower the unit cost of production. For example, as plants become larger, firms can exploit mass production techniques involving the specialization of labour on narrow specific tasks, the use of specialized machinery which is sometimes available only in very large minimum size, and so forth. To a large extent these economies are economies of large-scale plants. Empirical evidence indicates that these economies are not unlimited. Rather, over a range of increasing plant size, cost per unit tends to fall, but a critical size of plant is reached beyond which no further economies are likely to be encountered. This is often referred to as the minimum optimum scale. Sometimes optimum scales of output can be reached at several levels. For example, a study of the shoe industry in France has shown technical optima being reached at various plant scales, the competitive situation being unfavourable only at intermediate scales of output.

This evidence suggests, therefore, that although the existence of economies of large-scale production is not in doubt, caution is needed in dealing with claims relating to such economies. There is no guarantee that by concentrating European industry is inevitably going to become more efficient. It may become more efficient, provided that plants are of less than optimum size. On the other hand, it is possible that in some industries plants may already be near the optimum, or even at it, in which case there may be little or no opportunity for increased efficiency through greater size.

We might mention that in economic analysis the textbooks usually portray the average cost curve as being U-shaped. This suggests that increased size will carry with it greater efficiency, but that as a firm grows beyond a certain size it may in fact become absolutely less efficient. One reason for this could be that as the firm grows it eventually becomes more difficult to organize and manage, and thus dis-economies may begin to arise because of the unwieldy size. In the case of the European Community, this may not be merely an academic point. Much play has been made of the 'technological gap'. This has focused attention upon the inadequate R and D performance of European firms as compared with their American counterparts. But more recently stress has been laid upon the existence of a 'managerial gap'. That is to say, as compared with the US, the level of management ability in the Community is relatively low. It is therefore open to question whether management in the Community would necessarily be capable of administering the giant enterprises which the economies of scale (and R and D needs) might otherwise dictate. In other words, at present the size of firm and plant in the Community may be consonant with the general level of managerial ability which exists.

It is of course true that a firm may grow in size merely by duplicating optimal plants. There is, however, no guarantee that an increase in the size of firm brought about in this manner will give rise to greater economies. J. S. Bain tends to regard economies of multi-plant operation as being encountered in some but not all industries, and where encountered he tends to assign a relatively unimportant role to them. This may be true in the case of his sample, but there are cases where increased size does bring economies on the side of distribution. Firms can merge and eliminate overlapping sales activity; for example, the much publicized merger between Agfa of West Germany and Gevaert of Belgium led to very considerable concrete savings through the concentration of the two companies' world-wide sales networks.

Those who have sought to defend the greater concentration thesis have rested most of their case on the argument that Community enterprises are inferior in respect of their R and D efforts. A great deal has been made of the very great difference in the absolute volume of resources devoted to R and D in the US as compared with the Community. For example, in the year 1962 the amount expended on R and D in the US was more than four times that of the whole of the Community. Even if we allow for the fact that a straightforward exchange rate comparison is invalid (because R and D is a labour intensive activity) and we therefore apply a research exchange rate, it still appears that the US spent between two and three times as much as the Community. The relevance of this fact to the question of firm size would appear to be that small firms are not likely to engage in R and D, whereas larger ones can take on such a role. From this it is argued that European industry, being relatively small, is not in a position to carry out R and D on the same scale as American industry with its relatively large firms. This on the one hand, partly explains the great disparity in the amounts spent on R and D, and on the other is a potent cause of the superiority of American industry in international competition.

There is undoubtedly plenty of evidence to show that R and D is an activity which tends to increase with the size of firm. Thus, while it is unusual for firms of the smallest size to engage in research, it is just as unusual for firms of the largest size group not to do so, and the vast bulk of R and D spending is in fact carried out by firms in the larger size groups (see OECD, 1963). Nor is it difficult to show that those industries where R and D is particularly important are also those in which the US has, if not swept the board, at least taken an overwhelming lead. Thus in 1964 the US produced just over 80 per cent of the world output of electronic capital goods, i.e. electronic data-processing equipment, including computers; radar and navigational aids; radio communication and public broadcasting and transmitting equipment; electronic measuring, testing and analysing instruments; industrial and other electrical control equipment. The US was also responsible for 60 per cent of the exports of that output. In the computer field, one firm, IBM, holds a dominant position. It has been estimated that in 1964 62 per cent of all the new computer installations in Europe emanated from IBM (see Layton, 1966). The argument here is that competition in fields of this kind is based to an overwhelming extent on technological innovation and service to customers. The firms which succeed are those that can most rapidly develop a new product or an improved version of an existing one which renders current models obsolete. US lead-times, that is the periods between the preparation of product projects and delivery of the products to customers, are significantly faster than those of British industry, and there is no reason to believe that industry in the Six is any better than the British in this respect. The ability to get a product marketed quickly is facilitated, of course, by the greater R and D resources of US firms. They are prepared to throw everything in to get there first, and as a result the threshold (that is, the amount of money which must be spent per annum on R and D to stay in business on a long-term basis) in the electronics industry reflects this ability and willingness. Only firms which can match this kind of expenditure on a sustained basis can hope to stay in business on an independent footing. This is probably the most powerful argument in favour of the concentration thesis.

Of course, arguments can be advanced against this view. For example, it has been pointed out that it is by no means inevitable that the largest firms are responsible for the most intensive R and D efforts. A number of American studies demonstrate this. Thus Schmookler (1959) has cited evidence from a study of six US industries showing that in four cases the percentage of spending accounted for by R and D decreased in the largest firms. Another study of US industries, by Worley, (1961) measured research intensity by the proportion of total employees engaged on R and D work to the total employment of the firm, concluded that there was a tendency for firms near the middle of the distribution by size to hire relatively more R and D personnel than firms at either end. Mansfield (1964) has also provided further evidence which tends to support the views of Schmookler and Worley.

It may be questioned whether these critiques of size are relevant to the European economy today. Although the US studies show that the R and D intensity of the largest US firms tends to be less than that of merely large firms, it is important to bear in mind that thresholds are measured in absolute terms, and that a small proportion of a larger turnover devoted to R and D may pass over a threshold, whilst a higher proportion of a smaller turnover may not. Thus it follows that even if European firms did show a tendency for R and D intensities to decline as they grew in size, it might be necessary to accept such growth in order to match the absolute R and D efforts of US giants. There is, of course, a clear implication here for the maintenance of competition within the Community and this will be taken up later.

Adaptation of the business structure

It was indicated earlier that there are differences in the approach to the size problem adopted by various responsible bodies within the Community. The Commission of the EEC, while not denying that an increase in size may be required in some industries, has not taken the view that policy should be devoted entirely to bringing about a greater degree of concentration. The Commission's approach has been three-pronged. First, it has suggested that small firms might be able to make an impact in the field of R and D if they were to come together in joint research agreements. A number of firms could pool their resources for research purposes, and the results of such research would be available to all the participating firms. In implementation of this the Commission issued a notice on 23 July 1968 indicating its position on co-operative agreements between enterprises. The Commission takes the view that agreements relating to the joint execution of R and D work do not normally restrict competition. The Commission will therefore look upon them favourably. However, the Commission recognizes the possibility of infringements. For example, if enterprises

enter into commitments which restrict their own research and development activity or the utilization of the results of joint work so that they do not have a free hand with regard to their own research and development outside the joint projects, this can constitute an infringement of the rules of competition of the Treaties (EEC Commission, 1968b).

Second, on the specific question of concentration, the Commission has taken the view that the aim of policy should be to eliminate those factors that artifically encourage or impede concentration. Where economies of scale are as yet unreaped, the artificial factors that might inhibit their expansion should be eliminated. On the other hand, artificial factors that give rise to concentrated industrial structures even though no economies of scale exist should be swept away. The Commission has focused particular attention upon the fields of taxation and company law as ones in which conditions of neutrality should be brought about. In the fiscal field the most obvious distortion is the artificial stimulus to vertical concentration presented by the multi-stage or 'cascade' type of turnover taxes. These have existed in all the member states of the EEC except France, and have been particularly prominent in Germany. As we have seen, the 'cascade' system involves imposing a turnover tax upon raw materials, semi-finished products, or bought-in component parts every time they are sold by one firm to another. The result is that the taxes imposed in the earlier stages of manufacturing a product that passes through several stages are compounded in the final selling price of the product, which is thus higher than it would be but for the multiple incidence of tax. Under these circumstances, it is not surprising that industries in Germany should have chosen to avoid this multiple incidence wherever possible by vertical integration. In a completely vertically integrated concern that extends right back to the sources of raw materials, taxes are imposed only once at the final stage of production. The implications for the economy as a whole of this artificial inducement to vertical concentration are that the real economic advantages of specialization are less likely to be achieved, since the firm is encouraged to spread its activities for purely fiscal reasons, and vertical integration may in some circumstances make it possible for a vertically integrated concern to embarrass its non-integrated competitors, even if they are more efficient, by denying them raw materials, components or markets. The Commission has always held, therefore, that the solution to this problem lies in the adoption of the value-added system which has been operational in France. This form of tax neither encourages nor discourages vertical concentration. The Community has now decided to adopt this system, and therefore this problem of encouragement to vertical concentration will be dealt with in due course.

The other area where the EEC Commission has been seeking to bring about greater neutrality is in respect of company law, although it should be noted that in practice it is very difficult to separate the legal and the fiscal factors in operation here. The Commission recognizes that where greater business units are required one way of bringing them about is by merger. These mergers may take place within frontiers or may be cross-border in character. So far, however, the creation of the Common Market has not given rise to much business integration by genuine mergers between companies in different member-states. Examples, such as Agfa-Gevaert, are few indeed. Dutch experience indicates that Netherlands companies have been more inclined to merge with US, UK and Canadian enterprises than with companies in other EEC states. One explanation of the fewness of genuine cross-border mergers is that legal and fiscal obstacles make such amalgamations difficult and costly.

The nature of these inhibiting factors is best appreciated by considering what happens when two companies located in different member-states choose to merge. Suppose a Belgian and a German company decide to amalgamate and form a single company in Germany. Immediately, they face the problem that, under Belgian law, before the company can move out of Belgium it must have the unanimous consent of the shareholders. Where there are a lot of small shareholders, chances of unanimity are small. Some patriot is going to object. Moreover, under Belgian, German, French and Dutch law a domestic company cannot be absorbed by a foreign one in one simple move. For the above merger to occur, there has to be a legal liquidation in one country and a legal reconstruction in the other. Lawyers and registration fees naturally arise in the process. When a company is liquidated some countries impose a liquidation tax on the difference between the book value and the actual value of the company's assets. In addition, in most countries capital gains arising at the time of liquidation are subject to taxation. If the tax liability is substantial, it may make the cost of an amalgamation prohibitive.

Within each of the member-states of the EEC, therefore, the fiscal authorities make certain concessions to companies in these circumstances, perhaps by levying the tax at a reduced rate or by permitting the payment to be phased over a number of years. But this understanding attitude on the part of the authorities usually vanishes when cross-frontier amalgamations are under consideration. In particular, the possibility of phasing the tax payment over a number of years becomes unattractive to the official mind when the company on which the tax is levied is due to disappear from the national scene. Thus economically desirable mergers may be impeded.

Further obstacles can also arise. If an amalgamation takes the form of a parent in one country and a subsidiary in the other, the possibility of double taxation of dividends is a real one. Even in respect of national mergers, the fiscal systems of the Six only go part of the way toward eliminating this double taxation. In Germany, the Netherlands and Luxembourg, only when the degree of participation of the parent in the subsidiary is at least 25 per cent do companies enjoy the *schachtelprivileg* under which they are regarded by the fiscal authorities as part of a self-contained group, and double taxation of the subsidiaries' dividends is thus avoided.

To eliminate this obstacle and speed up the process of cross-border merger, two developments are needed. First, legal impediments should be removed, thus permitting companies to combine in a single company under a statute recognized by all Community countries – the so-called European company. Second, the fiscal factors that discriminate against cross-border mergers should be eliminated. If liquidation taxes are eliminated on domestic mergers, they should be dropped in respect of the cross-border variety also. Capital gain taxes on liquidation should be as liberally applied to cross-border mergers as they are to internal amalgamations. In some cases double-taxation conventions are needed.

Unfortunately, the European company has so far failed to materialize. This has apparently been due to a conflict between Gaullist nationalism and the European Commission. The French have proposed an identical body of law relating to European companies, to be introduced into each national legal system and interpreted by national courts. The Commission, on the other hand, would like to see European companies directly subject to a Community law that would be interpreted by the European Court of Justice. Despite these difficulties, preparatory work is being carried on. At present the Commission is preparing to ask the Council of Ministers to decide in principle in favour of a European-company convention. The Commission is proposing also to press the Council to take a number of decisions so that more detailed work can be carried out. The questions to be decided are as follows. Should European companies issue bearer shares that allow the identity of the owner to be unknown, or only registered shares? Should workers be allowed representation on boards of management? What would be the tax status of such companies? Which companies will be permitted to take on European company status? For example, will companies in the US be allowed access on equal terms with Community companies, without the need to operate through a subsidiary registered in the Six?

Cross-frontier amalgamations are of course attractive to the integrationist. Such business forms are adept at moving capital, manpower and 'know-how' across frontiers. They also have a political significance in that they constitute a built-in resistance to nationalistic policies. Of course it should be recognized that the EEC Commission may be unduly optimistic about the effectiveness of such legal and fiscal reforms in speeding the process of business integration within the Community. There are also psychological obstacles to cross-border mergers. People do not like to see their domestic companies swallowed up by foreign rivals[1] – one of the important features of the Agfa-Gevaert formula is that it preserves the identities of the parties to the original arrangement. Furthermore, even if companies can combine under a Community-wide company law, they will still have to face the fact that in dealings with debtors and so forth the law will differ from state to state. This is where the US has an advantage over the Community, since in the former although company

1. Member-state Governments are also reluctant to agree to mergers which may lead to R and D activity moving to another state. This appears to have explained the French Government's refusal to allow the Fiat Citroen merger.

law varies from state to state there is a single law of contract throughout the Union.

The Commission has also taken some steps to deal with the problem of the relatively low level of R and D spending as compared with the US. The medium-term policy committee has established a working group on scientific and technological research policy (formerly called the Groupe Marechal but now the Groupe Aigrain), whose first report was discussed by the Council of Ministers in October 1967. As a result of this report, the Council of Ministers of the EEC has laid down a programme of work for the co-ordination of national research policies in a number of fields: computers, telecommunications, new modes of transport, oceanography, metallurgy, loss of amenity, and meteorology. (More recently it has been proposed to the Community's five main computer producers – Philips, Siemens, Telefunken, Olivetti and the Compagnie International Informatique – that they should combine to build a data processing computer which would be competitive with US models.) The basic idea here is that not only private industry but also Governments are involved in R and D activity, and that the Community's limited R and D resources should be put to the best use. This can be achieved if unnecessary duplications of effort are eliminated. The idea of collaboration in order to minimize the dependence of Western Europe on the US has of course been a major factor inspiring the idea of a European Technological Community; this will be taken up in the next chapter.

At the national level the process of concentration has been taking place with Government encouragement. This is particularly true in the case of France. A prime aim of French policy in the Fifth Plan (1966–70) has been to reduce the number of independent enterprises by creating larger groups. In some cases it has been envisaged that only one or two firms should constitute the industry.

Anti-trust and the control of concentration

It is not difficult to see that the encouragement given to mergers at the national level and the search for more neutral conditions in respect of concentration at the Community level are bound sooner or later to create problems of an anti-trust character. Firms may expand by merger without there being any compensating economies arising from their greater size. Their growth may be largely dictated by the desire either to exploit their market power or to establish a position in which they can lead a relatively quiet life. When greater economies arise, a market-power problem may also exist. In the latter case, at least some degree of supervision may be called for.

Before pursuing this problem further, it is necessary to recognize that the basic act of creating one large Common Market out of six previously separate national economies vastly increases the area over which firms face competition, and therefore correspondingly reduces the possibility of market domination by particular enterprises. With a large market firms can usually grow considerably in size without any problem of oligopoly or monopoly arising at all. This is why, in the majority of cases, the European Commission feels that mergers are to be welcomed without reservation in the present context of European integration. Having a large market, whether European or American, means that effective competition and really big businesses – uneasy or even incompatible bed-fellows within a small national market with high tariffs – usually become simultaneously feasible. Nevertheless, eventually the process of concentration is bound to create problems, and in a limited number of cases such problems may be imminent.

It should also be borne in mind that although the creation of a large Community market appears to stave off the market domination problem, this is only true in so far as the process of integrating markets is really carried out in a thorough-going fashion. It is true that tariffs have been eliminated and quotas have likewise been swept away. But before goods can move freely and markets are thoroughly integrated, many other obstacles have to be dealt with. For example, it is common for Governments to insist upon laying down technical standards, and these differ materially from one country to another. It is only when these obstacles to the free movement of goods have been eliminated that the concentrated enterprises in particular national markets are subjected to competition from firms outside.

As we have already seen, because of the need to control concentration, and therefore preserve the competition which has been a goal both in the ECSC and in the EEC, those who drafted the Paris and Rome Treaties provided powers to deal with the concentration problem. In the case of the Paris Treaty, the powers which were conferred upon the High Authority are particularly impressive. (In some degree, these powers reflect the fact that the Treaty was drafted at the time when the US was a major occupying power in West Germany. A prominent feature of Allied policy, largely under American inspiration, was deconcentration activity in German heavy industry.) The Treaty requires that all mergers or other forms of concentration shall be notified to the High Authority and approved by it before being implemented. Approval must be refused in any case that would seriously reduce effective competition in the markets of the coal and steel products. This relatively severe policy is reminiscent of the US Clayton Act, although it must be admitted that in practice the High Authority has not been particularly impressive in using the powers given to it.

We have also seen that the Rome Treaty deals with the problem of concentrated enterprises, but the approach is significantly different from that of the ECSC. Article 86 of the Treaty can be summarized very simply as follows: abuse of a dominant position in the Common Market, or in a substantial part thereof, is prohibited if trade between the member-states is affected. If these conditions are simultaneously fulfilled, the practice in question is illegal. This Article provides no general power to prohibit mergers. The Commission is given the power to deal with abuse of a dominant position, but not to prevent a dominant position from coming about. This is a basic weakness of the Rome Treaty. Ideally the European Commission should be able to prevent positions of market power from arising in the first instance. It is not desirable to allow such positions of power to emerge, since it is far from easy to break up dominant enterprises once they have come into existence. This is particularly true in the case of the Six, where there is no tradition of vigorous anti-trust policy.

The fact that the Rome Treaty, as generally interpreted at present, confers no power in respect of mergers poses a serious problem, and it is one which has been engaging the attention of the EEC Commission. Two possible solutions are under consideration; one is to try to extend the interpretation of Article 86 to cover mergers; the second is to take over some of the powers which were conferred upon the High Authority. The first solution is far from ideal. There are circumstances where it may be possible for the Commission to interpret Article 86 in a way which would enable it to prevent a merger. However, the Commission is only likely to be able to act when one of the enterprises involved in a concentration is already in a dominant position. The second alternative is therefore the more promising. It is proposed that the three Community Treaties eventually be fused. When this occurs the possibility exists that the power to veto mergers, which at present applies only to coal and steel, could be extended to all Community products and services.

From what has gone before, it is apparent that there are two strands in the concentration policy of the Six. One consists of encouraging the concentration process, or at least neutralizing some of the forces which bear upon it. National encouragement, at least in the case of France, has proceeded apace and successfully. The Community policy of neutrality has scored one success in that the value-added tax will be standard throughout the Six. But the European company, though generally recognized to be a necessity, is still some way off. As for making the R and D efforts of the Six as effective as possible, it seems likely that a favourable regime for co-operative agreements will yield more fruit than Government confrontations.

The other strand consists of increasing the powers of the Commission to deal with mergers. To the student of anti-trust this seems an absolute necessity, but it is doubtful that the French will look kindly upon it. A salient point is that since the US market is more than twice the size of that of the Six, in so far as Community firms emulate their rivals in size the degree of concentration in the Six will become greater than that in the US. This fact should spur the Six on to recognized that development of an effective method of merger control is not indefinitely postponable.

8 The Community and the World

The subject of the Community's relations with the rest of the world can best be treated under three heads. The first form of relationship is that of association. The Rome Treaty made special provision for the dependent territories of member-states. The possibility of association was not, however, limited to dependent or erstwhile dependent territories. The second form of relationship is full membership; this will be discussed at some length in the light of the particular interest which the UK has had and still has in the subject. Thirdly, the Rome Treaty calls for a common commercial policy. This in particular provides an opportunity to discuss the activities of the Community in the GATT.

Association

During the negotiations leading up to the Rome Treaty the French vigorously pressed the idea of associating overseas territories. The Spaak Report made no mention of them and it was only at the Venice meeting of foreign ministers in May 1956 that France, by making association a condition of going ahead with the scheme for a Common Market, got the subject on the agenda. The French had good reasons for taking this line. Firstly, they regarded the overseas territories as an extension of France, but a customs union of the Six would definitely discriminate against them. Secondly, France bore a considerable burden both in the form of aid and relatively high prices for colonial raw materials. She felt that the Six should be placed on a more equal footing by taking on part of the financial responsibility. This was further emphasized by the fact that countries such as Germany were investing in commercial enterprises in the French dependencies and therefore derived much advantage from French expenditure on the necessary infrastructures. Part Four of the Treaty (Articles 131–6) specifically relates to the overseas dependencies. They were listed in Annex IV and included French West Africa, French Equatorial Africa, the French Trustee territory in the Cameroons,

Madagascar, a range of other French overseas settlements and Togoland, the Belgian Congo and Ruandra Urundi, the Italian Trustee territory of Somalia and Netherlands New Guinea. The Netherlands Antilles was added in 1964.

The original basis of association was concluded for five years. Essentially it had a double character. The Community undertook to reduce its tariffs on goods coming from the dependencies in line with internal tariff disarmament. This was a vital concession in so far as the primary products supplied by non-Associated states faced the Community's common external tariff. The dependent territories were required to reciprocate but could, however, retain protection needed for their development, industrialization or revenue, provided they extended to all member-states the preferences they had previously extended to the mother country. The Treaty also brought into existence the European Development Fund (EDF) which was to channel aid to the associated territories. The Six agreed that over the first five years they would make available $581·25 million. France and West Germany subcribed $200 million, Italy $40 million, Belgium and the Netherlands $70 million each and Luxembourg $1·75 million. French territories obtained no less than $511·25 million of this aid. It should perhaps be added that owing to administrative and technical difficulties there was a considerable delay in disbursing this money.

By 1960, many of the overseas territories had become independent and a new basis of association was required. Therefore in 1961 and 1962 negotiations took place which lead to the Yaoundé Convention. This was signed on 20 July 1963 and came into effect, for a further period of five years, on 1 June 1964. It covered eighteen associated states, namely, Burundi, Cameroon, the Central African Republic, Chad, Congo (Kinshasa), Congo (Brazzaville), Dahomey, Gabon, Upper Volta, the Ivory Coast, Madagascar, Mali, Mauritania, Niger, Rwanda, Senegal, Somalia and Togo. The Convention also extended to Surinam, the Netherlands Antilles and French overseas territories and departments. Because of the criticism of non-associated primary producing countries the preference accorded to associated states was reduced by lowering the common external tariff on some tropical products.

As a concession, the aid from the EDF was stepped up to $730 million and a further $70 million was to be made available by the European Investment Bank (EIB) for French and Dutch non-self-governing territories and for French overseas departments. As in the first association arrangement, firms of the member-states enjoyed the right of free establishment in the associates and free movement of capital was provided for. However, unlike the first arrangement, the Yaoundé Convention also created an institutional framework including a Council of Ministers.

Inevitably, the preferences granted to the associated states have given rise to criticism. The Latin American States have persistently called upon the EEC to abolish the preferential system. Raoul Prebisch, when Secretary General of UNCTAD, launched vigorous attacks on the system and as a result the EEC showed itself prepared to make concessions at the second UNCTAD at New Delhi in 1968. However, it ought to be added that the preferences enjoyed by virtue of association have not enabled the associates to expand their exports to the Six more rapidly than the developing world as a whole. Indeed, between 1958 and 1967 whereas the exports of the associates increased by 47 per cent, the figure for the developing world as a whole increased by 68 per cent. In 1969 the Yaoundé Convention was renewed and the present arrangement governs the aid and trade relationships between the eighteen and the Six until 31 January 1975. Two points in the new agreement are worth noting. The minimum level of aid was $1000 million although $82 million of this was for the associated overseas departments and territories of member-states. Also, following undertakings at the second UNCTAD, it was agreed that the common external tariff towards third countries generally on tropical products should be reduced. As a consolation the associates are to benefit from a reduction in the defences for Community agricultural producers under the common agricultural policy.

So far the discussion has been about the association provisions designed originally for the Community's colonial dependencies. In addition Article 238 provides for association with third countries generally. The first two countries to take advantage of this provision were Greece and Turkey. The Greek Treaty of

Association began operation on 1 November 1962. Under it a customs union was to be founded between the Six and Greece over a period of twelve years. This involved Greece in accepting the common external tariff. The cuts in tariffs on intra-Community trade were extended to Community imports of Greek goods. On the other hand, Greece had twelve years to remove her tariffs on Community goods. Moreover, in respect of industrial goods, which constituted about a third of the Greek imports, Greece was allowed twenty-two years to eliminate tariffs. This was specifically designed to enable Greek industry to develop to a state where it would face Community industry on equal terms. The association agreement also provided for $125 million of loans from the EIB over the first five years. Apparently, up to the end of 1966 only $63 million had been lent and this led to some dissatisfaction on the part of the Greeks. Provision was also made for the gradual harmonization of Greek agricultural, economic and trade policies with those of the Community. The Treaty also envisaged the eventual prospect of full membership of the Community. The Turkish association began operating on 1 December 1964. Under the Treaty a five-year (extendable to nine or more years) preparatory period was provided for which was aimed at strengthening the Turkish economy. Imports into the Community of four Turkish crops (tobacco, dried figs, raisins and hazelnuts), which provided about 40 per cent of Turkish export earnings, were to benefit from tariff free quotas which were subsequently increased. Also during the five-year preparatory period the EIB was to lend $67 million for Turkish development. The preparatory period was to be followed by a twelve-year transition period during which a customs union would be established between the Six and Turkey. Over this period Turkish economic policy was to be harmonized with that of the Community and as in the case of Greek association the possibility of eventual full membership was held out. By and large the Turks seem to have found their arrangement satisfactory.

Other states have been attracted by the possibilities of association. When the Yaoundé Convention was signed a statement was issued indicating the willingness of the Community to give favourable consideration to requests for association from countries in similar economic situations to those already associated. This point was taken up by Nigeria. As a result an Association Treaty was signed in Lagos in June 1966. Under it Nigerian goods were to be accorded the same terms of entry into the Community market as were granted to the eighteen Yaoundé Convention states except for certain goods in respect of which import quotas were agreed. In return Nigera undertook to grant duty free entry to Community goods. However, she undertook to avoid discrimination against non-Community countries by changing her customs duties to fiscal duties and charging these on Community goods. In respect of imports of twenty-six products a small customs duty was to be levied but this was not to apply to Community goods. The entry into force of the association could only occur after ratification by all the contracting parties. This process was delayed by political factors and at the end of May 1969 the Treaty was due to expire simultaneously with the Yaoundé Convention. Austria, with the agreement of the EFTA, has been seeking an association with the Community. Under the State Treaty of 1955 Article 4 precludes any form of economic union with West Germany and as a result association is all that Austria can aim for. Since 1964 the Maghreb States (Algeria, Morocco and Tunisia) have also been seeking associate status. Non-discriminatory trade agreements have been signed with Iran, Lebanon and Israel, although the latter would prefer associate status. Finally, it should be mentioned that under the Arusha Accord of 1968, Kenya, Uganda and Tanzania signed an association agreement with the Community.

Membership

Article 237 of the Rome Treaty declares that any European state may apply to become a member. Unanimous agreement is required within the Council of Ministers before a state can be admitted – this explains the ability of the French to veto British membership.

Until quite late in the 1950s various British Ministers went on record as saying that the UK could never become a full member of the Community. As we have seen, a number of factors were adduced in support of this view. The first was the effect upon the Commonwealth. Commonwealth preference would have to give way to the common external tariff. This would harm Commonwealth members at a time when the idea of a multi-lingual, multiracial Commonwealth was still on the lips of most politicians and was still regarded as an important vehicle of British influence. Also, the elimination of Commonwealth countries' preferences in the British market was almost certainly likely to lead to a loss of British preferences in Commonwealth markets. There were also some specific problems. One was that New Zealand relied heavily on the UK as an outlet for her butter production. The other was the British import of sugar from low-income Commonwealth countries under the Commonwealth Sugar Agreement. Secondly, there was the British agricultural system. It was supported in a radically different way from that adopted on the Continent. The level of farm incomes and the participation of farmers in price determination were at stake. Also, as we shall see later, the adoption of a Community system was bound to raise prices and the food import bill. Thirdly, the formation of the EFTA raised the problem that British membership of the Community would require that adequate arrangements be made for our EFTA partners. Then finally there was the critical point of supra-nationalism. The need to give up sovereignty was not welcomed then and it has remained a subject upon which British politicians still tend to be wary. (It is not beyond the bounds of possibility that political rather than economic matters could ultimately prove to be the achilles heel of Britain's membership bid.)

However, it was apparent by 1960 that the Conservative Government was beginning to change its tune and in the House of Commons on 31 July 1961 Mr Macmillan, the Prime Minister, formally announced that the UK had decided to apply for full membership. A letter to this effect was sent on 9 August 1961. The Irish Republic despatched its request before the UK – on the day of the House of Commons announcement. Denmark's application was despatched the day after the UK's. Norway, however, waited until 1962 before applying. Subsequently Austria, Sweden and Switzerland made separate applications for association. Portugal also applied, though no clear indication was given of the arrangement sought. The Council of Ministers decided to accept the British application of 26 September 1961 and on 10 October of the same year the UK, through Mr Edward Heath, made a comprehensive statement of its position at a Ministerial Conference in Paris. The negotiations which subsequently followed dragged on until 14 January 1963 when General de Gaulle at a Paris Press Conference declared that Britain was not ripe for membership and it was left to M. Maurice Couve de Murville to deliver a *coup de grace* on 29 January at Brussels by securing the indefinite adjournment of negotiations.

The issues involved in the negotiations were extremely complex. Basically the origin of the problem was quite simple. Britain did not approach with a view to signing the Rome Treaty as it stood. Rather, because of her commitment to the Commonwealth and the EFTA, as well as her different farming system, she sought modifications and accommodations on most fronts.

In the short space available the issues involved can be sketched only in outline. On the agricultural front Mr Heath admitted that the UK would have to move over to the EEC system. One of the main areas of conflict here was the speed of transition. The UK thought in terms of a transition period of up to twelve to fifteen years, but the Six were adamant that the common agricultural policy would have to be applied in its entirety by the end of the Treaty transition period. On the question of a need for an annual farm price review the UK obtained a tolerably satisfactory solution.

The major problems of the Commonwealth sprang from protection which the Community was destined to place around itself when the common external tariff and the common agricultural policy were fully operational. The UK accepted that the common external tariff was a *fait accompli* but called for a 20 per cent cut. The UK also called for nil duties on twenty-six industrial products. Progress on this issue was slow. By the time of the suspension of negotiations only ten products had been dealt with, some on the basis of nil solutions but others by virtue of the UK withdrawing its request and accepting a form of transitional provision. On the subject of industrial goods produced by Canada, Australia and New Zealand, the UK recognized that the common external tariff would have to be applied and an agreement was reached on its application in stages and full operation by 1970.

The Community did, however, declare its willingness in 1966 and 1969 to examine the possibility of developing trade with these countries. In the case of processed foodstuffs, Britain produced a list of eighty products which were regarded as being entitled to nil duty or preferential measures. In practice in the case of half it was decided to apply the common external tariff at the same rate as industrial goods, but in the case of the other half a more gradual alignment was agreed.

One of the most acute Commonwealth problems arose in connexion with temperate foodstuffs. Britain proposed that once she was within the Community the latter should provide comparable outlets to those which temperate food producers had enjoyed previously. The Six, however, were adamant that they could offer no permanent or indeed long-term guarantee to Commonwealth producers. They were prepared to negotiate specific and limited agreements but permanent solutions would have to be sought in the framework of world-wide agreements. New Zealand was regarded as meriting exceptional treatment as regards butter but no solution in terms of guarantees was achieved.

In the case of India, Pakistan, Ceylon and Hong Kong the general solution was twofold. Firstly, there was to be a very gradual application of the common external tariff but with special treatment in certain cases. Thus, in the case of tea there was to be a nil duty and in other cases there was to be an indefinite suspension of duties. Secondly, the Community would negotiate comprehensive trade agreements with India and Pakistan in order to guarantee or indeed increase their foreign currency earnings. For cotton goods special agreements would be made to ensure that exports to the enlarged Community were not harmed.

In the case of other less developed countries in Africa and the West Indies, the UK hoped that they would be able to take advantage of the association provisions. Nigeria, Ghana and Tanganyika, however, disliked the political overtones and declined this offer. The Commission countered by offering either participation in a new Yaoundé Convention (an arrangement which acknowledged independence of what where formerly colonial dependencies) or specific trade agreements.

The solution to the EFTA problem lay in the participants either becoming full or associate members. Three took one course and three the other, whilst Portugal's intentions were unclear. At the time when the UK negotiations were suspended the negotiations with Norway and Denmark were advanced. Formal talks on the Irish application had hardly begun. In the case of the three applicants for association the first round of talks to ascertain the problems to be dealt with had taken place between the EEC Commission and a delegation from the country concerned, and on this basis the Commission had reported to the Council. But no formal negotiations had been opened.

As already indicated, negotiations were abruptly terminated by General de Gaulle. Britain was an independent maritime power not yet sufficiently European to be admitted. This was a half-truth. The fact that she had applied indicated a new European emphasis in foreign policy. The fact that she did not merely accept the Treaty but sought to negotiate so many modifications in the interests of the Commonwealth was a reflection of the fact that her imperial past, although no longer a dominating interest, still exercised a significant constraint on policy. There can be no doubt that the arduous negotiations arising out of the need to seek special treatment on products as divergent as kangaroo meat and cricket bats played into the hands of the French. But the real root of French opposition was undoubtedly political. Firstly, Britain would be an American 'trojan horse'. Secondly, in a Community of ten, French influence would be watered down.

Having laid the blame largely at the door of the French, it is fair to ask whether the negotiations could have succeeded. The general impression of the delegations, except the French, was that there was a good chance of reaching a successful conclusion if the negotiations had continued. Professor Hallstein, President of the Commission at the time, was more guarded. Speaking before the European Parliament in 1963 he observed

it is not possible to say of the negotiations at the moment when they were interrupted that they had in practice failed, or to say that it had been proved that they could succeed (quoted in Palmer *et al.*, 1968, p. 243).

The change of Government in the UK did not, however, change the course of British policy, since the Labour Party itself became convinced of the need for the UK to join the Community. On 10 November 1966 the Prime Minister, Harold Wilson, announced to the House of Commons plans for a high-level approach to the Six with the intention of becoming a full member of the Community. This was followed between January and March 1967 by visits to the capitals of the Six. Having judged the prospects to be satisfactory, the Prime Minister announced to the House of Commons on 2 May that the UK would submit its second application. This was made on 11 May and was followed by applications from Ireland, Denmark and Norway.

The British approach on this occasion was radically different to that of the 1961-3 period. No attempt was going to be made to secure a multitude of accommodations and concessions. The areas for negotiation were reduced to these. The common agricultural policy was bound to have a substantial repercussion on the balance-of-payments and cost of living. The basis of the policy was accepted but an adequate transition period was required. Also a more equitable sharing of the financial burdens of the policy would be necessary. A comprehensive annual review of the agricultural industry should be held, broadly similar to that introduced within the Community but with agricultural producers' organizations formally participating in the review procedure. There were some Commonwealth interests which needed safeguarding and in particular New Zealand and the sugar producers. The problem of capital movements would also require attention. The UK stance also differed in that on this occasion it claimed that it would bring with it a dowry in the form of its considerable achievements and potential in the field of science and technology. The latter led to suggestions about a new Community – the European Technological Community. The British bid was also sweetened, although somewhat vaguely, by references to Britain's awareness of the possibility of progress towards political unity.

The application for membership was examined by the Council of Ministers on 10 July 1967 and the Council decided to obtain the opinion of the Commission. The Commission presented its conclusions in September. It noted that views differed as to the priorities that were given to solving the Community's own internal problems as opposed to solving the problems inherent in an extension of the Community. It recommended that an attempt be made to deal with both simultaneously and that negotiations should be opened. The Commission did, however, note the urgent need to solve the British balance-of-payments problem and to adjust the role of sterling so that it could be fitted into a Community monetary system. The reference to the problem caused by sterling was an entirely new and indeed ominous feature of the UK–EEC dialogue. As one observer has remarked of the previous negotiations

In those long weeks . . . in Brussels in 1962, everything else was gone into – every detail of Commonwealth trade from carpets to kangaroo tails – but never a word about sterling (Strange, 1967).

In October and November the question of negotiations were discussed by the Council of Ministers without result. In November the Prime Minister re-emphasized the UK's technical dowry, proposing a seven-point plan for European technology. These covered bilateral projects with other European partners, multilateral discussions on improving Europe's technological capability, the establishment of a European Technological Institute as well as offers to co-operate in the field of European business mergers, company law, and patents. However, later that month General de Gaulle delivered another of his famous press conferences which effectively closed the door to entry. The General took the view that full membership for Britain would lead to the destruction of the Community. Some form of association would, however, be acceptable. Great play was made of the British balance-of-payments deficit which was said to indicate a permanent state of disequilibrium. The restrictions on the export of capital by the UK were contrasted with free movement within the Six. Then there was the sterling system with its large and vulnerable liabilities. At the Ministerial meeting on 19 December 1967, the Five expressed themselves in favour of commencing negotiations but France took the view that enlargement would profoundly modify the nature and ways of administering the Community.

In addition, the UK economy had to be restored to health before its application could be considered. No vote was taken. The Community once more agreed to disagree and the application remained on the agenda.

Subsequently, various member-states put forward proposals to bring the UK closer to the Community and prepare her for membership. The Commission lent a hand by proposing a preferential trade arrangement with the states seeking membership, together with closer consultation and collaboration on scientific and technological matters. No progress was made. However, the events of May 1968 and the resignation of General de Gaulle in 1969 brought the subject of British membership back into the foreground. At the time of writing the leaders of the three main British parties are united on the membership issue and the Six are agreed on negotiations.

Common Market Pros and Cons

Having discussed the history of the membership issue and referred to some of the obstacles and difficulties which have been encountered, two topics clearly suggest themselves for discussion. What are the advantages and disadvantages of membership? Is Common Market membership the only alternative to the present state of things?

Any discussion of pros and cons has to begin by recognizing that the matter is political as well as economic. Whereas to a limited degree the economic aspects can be quantified in money terms and some attempt can be made to set off the advantages against disadvantages, the political aspects cannot be quantified at all precisely and certainly not in money terms. This makes the task of ultimate assessment extremely difficult. On the economic side, it has already been implied that the arguments do not all point in one direction. Whichever way the argument goes, it is, so to speak, an argument on balance. It also appears that the cons are more easily quantifiable than the pros. In other words, the cost of the balance of payments and the rise in the cost of living are relatively easily quantifiable by comparison with measuring the effects of industrial free trade such as the stimulus of competition, the opportunities to enjoy more fully the economies of scale and the possibilities of greater technological collaboration.

Undoubtedly the major problem is associated with agriculture. Basically it has three aspects. The first relates to the balance of payments. Since the UK imports a substantial part of its food requirements, membership of the Common Market would involve a rise in our food import bill. If we import food from the Community it would have to be bought at relatively high Common Market prices and there would be an immediate loss across the exchanges. If on the food we imported from the Commonwealth levies and the like were applied, most of them would in the first instance accrue to the Community and not to the UK. The second aspect is immediately apparent – the price of food would rise and thus the cost of living index. (The saving on farm subsidies would of course enable the Government to help the lower income group hit by rising prices.) This in turn could cause a sympathetic rise in wage rates and therefore costs and prices. British exports could be disadvantaged, although a compensating movement of the exchange rate could be introduced. The third aspect is that British farmers would be subject to Common Market prices for food produce and they might find them less advantageous than those stemming from the UK's Annual Farm Price Review. Strictly speaking, prices are not an important thing to farmers. Rather, like the rest of us, it is their incomes which matter and these would depend upon the volume of output which could be sold and the cost of inputs (some of which are other farmers' outputs) as well as prices. It should also be pointed out that unlike the first two aspects, a farm-income problem is not an inevitable consequence of membership.

Various calculations of the impact of the common agricultural policy have been made. Some are private but workmanlike, some are official – both deserve serious attention. Others consist of relatively simple calculations by press commentators or are said to be officially inspired leakages in the press. These latter need to be treated with considerable reserve although they cannot be dismissed out of hand. Usually these latter two categories suggests the highest cost of entry.

A calculation by T. K. Warley (1967) of the projected cost to the balance of payments, which took account of what the structure of output and consumption at common prices would be, suggested a cost of £212 million although as he observed:

The unseemly spectacle of arbitrary assumptions being piled upon conjecture will serve to convince the reader of the view that the balance-of-payments cost to Britain of applying the CAP cannot really be estimated within even tolerably confident limits.

On the subject of the rise in food prices, Warley's calculations forecasted a rise of 8 per cent and an increase in the cost-of-living index of 2·5 per cent. The UK Government at the time of the 1966–7 initiative produced its own calculations of the impact on the balance of payments and cost of living. It suggested a balance-of-payments cost of between £75–£250 million, a rise in the cost of food of 10–14 per cent and a rise in the cost of living index of $2\frac{1}{2}$–$3\frac{1}{2}$ per cent. The CBI (1966) also produced its own calculations which suggested a balance-of-payments cost of £250 million.

Then in 1970 the UK Government produced its White Paper – *Britain and the European Communities: An Economic Assessment* (Cmnd 4289) – which contained yet further calculations. The main effect of the White Paper was to plunge the whole subject into even greater obscurity. The range of possible impacts was extremely wide, and both pro and anti 'marketeers' could draw sustenance from it. The White Paper attempted to assess the total impact of membership and therefore took account not only of agriculture but also of capital movements, invisible and visible trading items. The upshot was that the cost to the balance-of-payments of all these factors could be as little as £100 million of as much as £1100 million. On the food and agriculture side the effect on the retail cost of food would be an increase of 18–26 per cent with a consequent rise in the general cost-of-living index of 4–5 per cent. The rise might, however, be spread over a transition period which might end in 1978. It is important to note that the British consumer would not necessarily escape the whole of this rise in food prices if the UK stayed outside the EEC since food can be expected to become more expensive in any event.

On the balance-of-payments implications of agricultural policy the White Paper makes three calculations. The first is the change in the cost of our food imports when inside the Community. The second is our contribution to the Community's agricultural budget. The third is concerned with the size of the funds received back from the Community Agricultural Fund by British farmers. In order to arrive at an answer to the first question some estimate is necessary of the extent to which the value of British food imports might be reduced because British farmers produced more at home, or might be increased because higher prices from Europe did not cut back consumption. The optimistic conclusion of the White Paper is a fall in the import bill of £85 million – the pessimistic one is an increase of £255 million. The *Economist* in its observations on the subject (14 February 1970) took the view that even the optimistic assessment was too low and suggested that a £100 million improvement was likely. On the subject of the contribution to the agricultural budget the optimistic estimate was a cost of £150 million but the pessimistic view envisaged a £670 million drain. The *Economist*'s observation on this point is highly relevant. It pointed out that if the UK paid £670 million it would indeed contribute as much as the rest of the EEC put together. Indeed £670 million is ridiculously high and if the UK share was 20 per cent a figure of £350 would be implied. (The *Economist*'s standpoint is supported by a report from Edgard Pisani (1969), a former French Minister of Agriculture, to the Action Committee for the United States of Europe which indicated that under the then existing financial rules the UK would have to bear more than 50 per cent of joint expenditure on agriculture. This would be unfair as UK national income would only be 25 per cent of the national income of a seven-member Community (Pisani, 1969). It would therefore be reasonable for the UK to seek to reduce this burden either by putting less into the central fund or by getting more out of it.) On the subject of UK farmers' receipts from the Fund the figures ranged between £100 million and £50 million. On the agricultural side therefore the White Paper's overall pessimistic conclusion was a balance-of-payments debit of £875 million and on the optimistic side a debit of £35 million. The *Economist*, however, and with some justification, assessed the debit as £175 million. The latter figure suggests that the costs might not be greatly different from those calculated by Warley and the Government in 1967. Plainly with such uncertainty the simplest answer is to negotiate and find out. There is of course no doubt that agriculture is bound to be a debit item. In so far as the UK views the pros and cons of EEC membership in economic terms only there is therefore a need to find a significant economic credit item.

Before passing on, some account should be taken of the effects on the farming community itself. In 1967 Warley calculated that gross farming income would be about 2 per cent lower if the UK was in the EEC than if it was outside. Although he argued that net farm income might not drop by this amount he concluded

... the result would not then support the view that British agriculture as a whole would be better off under the CAP given its present broad pattern of output and resource employment, especially as it could be expected that fertilizer would represent a loss to the industry at current rates of expenditure of a further £40m. (Warley, 1967, p. 47).

This conclusion was, however, reached before the 1967 devaluation. Since the common-policy prices are fixed in terms of a unit of account, devaluation automatically raised the sterling price which would be enjoyed by UK farmers. In the light of this Warley subsequently observed

... it would seem that some of the adverse effects on the incomes of British farmers of having to accept EEC prices would be considerably less acute at the new rate of exchange. Though there would still be difficult adjustment problems for some sectors, notably horticulturists and producers of store lambs, eggs and pigmeat, products which would have been marginally less profitable at the former exchange rate (e.g. milk, sugar beet) would now be more profitable than at current British prices, and producers of cereals and beef would enjoy even higher profits under the CAP (Warley, 1969, p. 304).

Returning now to the balance of payments there are two other disadvantages which need to be mentioned. One is that British exports would almost certainly lose their preferences in Commonwealth markets. However, this would not be disastrous since, as the NEDC pointed out, the Commonwealth countries have in any case been whittling our preferences away. The other point is that liberalization of capital movements could pose a problem. Professor H. G. Johnson has recently commented on this problem as follows:

Estimates of the probable effects of liberalization of capital movements on the British balance of payments are difficult to make with any confidence and have ranged from £100 to £300 million additional outflow per year. There are really two sorts of problems here, each dependent on terminating the chronic weakness of the British balance of payments. The first is that liberalization of capital movements would widen the scope for capital flights promoted by lack of confidence in sterling; this problem would become manageable if Britain were able to establish a stronger balance-of-payments position. The second is that of a larger flow of long-term capital to Europe in the form of portfolio and direct investment. If it were not for the balance-of-payments problem, such an increased flow might be balanced by a reverse flow of European capital to Britain, or a larger flow into Britain from outside to take advantage of opportunities created by British membership in the EEC, or both; in any case, whether they were balanced by inflows or not, such flows would represent the beneficial results of a quest to find the most profitable opportunities for the investment of British financial and industrial capital (Johnson, 1969, p. 24).

The White Paper too recognized that capital movements would involve a sizeable cost to the balance of payments although on the other hand invisible earnings would benefit from membership. However, it is important not to take too pessimistic a view of the capital-movements problem. There is a tendency to assume that the Six, and the Brussels Commission in particular, will apply Community rules in an inflexible and bureaucratic manner. It can be argued that if the UK encounters difficulties in this field then accommodations could be sought. In this respect we have to take note of the degree to which France has been allowed, particularly since May 1968, to take protective measures.

We turn now to the advantages. It is easy to see that British industrial exports could be boosted by no longer having to climb over the common external tariff hurdle. On the other hand, the protection hitherto enjoyed by the UK against Common Market manufactures would be swept away and as a result there would be an increase in UK imports. There are two ways of looking at this kind of problem – one is the static welfare effects, the other is the effect on the trade balance. In respect of the former, Professor Johnson (1969, p. 23) is on record as saying that no scientifically satisfactory estimates of the static welfare effects of British membership of the EEC have yet been produced. However, in 1958 his calculations of the advantages of joining the EEC – on the assumption that Britain had entered the EEC in its early stages – were put at 1 per cent of the assumed Gross National Product of 1970 (Johnson, 1958, p. 255). (This study appears to have related purely to trade in manufactures.) Indeed generally the static gains are thought to be small. From the point of view of the trade balance it must be admitted that the evidence is conflicting. The White Paper envisaged a debit item of between £125 million and £275 million. The detailed evidence supporting these calculations is not, however, revealed and, for what it is worth, The *Economist* described the figures as 'unadulterated rubbish'. In contrast, as we shall see later, a study by Maxwell Stamp Associates (1967) has suggested an increase of exports of manufactures over imports of $221 million.

Returning now to the static gains, it must be pointed out that the smallness of them does not mean that the matter ends there. Rather, the proponents of membership argue that it is in the field of dynamic factors that the advantages are to be found.

One such advantage is the economies of large-scale production. To the extent that national markets are not sufficiently large to reap the full benefit of such economies, there is a case for the larger market. It should be added that the problem is not just one of whether UK industry can reap such economies. In so far as Common Market membership leads to a growing amount of trade between the UK and the rest of the Community, it is important that German industry, for example, should be able to reap such economies since we are purchasing their goods. It can, of course, be argued that the UK market will usually be big enough to accommodate one plant of optimum size. Against this it needs to be pointed out that ideally it is necessary not only to have firms with optimum plants but also firms in competition. This becomes much more of a possibility within a common market consisting of the Six and the Seven plus the Irish Republic.

Perhaps more important than the economies of large-scale production is the fact that in some important industries survival depends on being able to mount the kind of annual R and D expenditures which are customary among the giant US enterprises. Thus Lord Plowden, Chairman of Tube Investments, and Professor Karl Winnacker, Chairman of Hoechst, in a report to the Action Committee for the United States of Europe point out the following in the case of the computer industry.

In terms of the value of installed computers, the American IBM concern, for example, supplies over two-thirds of the European market. In the list of the largest computer manufacturers such as IBM, Univac, Control Data, General Electric, Honeywell, and many others, European concerns are completely absent. Of a total of about 8000 computers installed in the EEC, the IBM, Bull/General Electric and Univac models accounted for about 52 per cent, 18 per cent and 8 per cent respectively (Plowden and Winnacker, 1969).

Clearly there is a case for the creation of larger units which can compete with American industry. If such large units are to exist, then an enlarged market is almost inevitably necessary if the heavy R and D expenditures are to be spread over a large volume of output, and if we are to have competition. In so far as within the enlarged market progress is made on such matters as the European company then the creation of such units will be facilitated whilst the choice of partners will be greater than at the national level. (It has indeed been suggested that there should be a European IRC to arrange the necessary marriages.)[1]

It is also necessary to take notice of the fact that Governments are involved in R and D. The Concorde is an example of the fact that some technological developments which are beyond the means of private industry can also strain the finances of individual Governments. In short, in partnership with the other members it would be possible to have a stake in technological ventures which the UK could not afford to embark on alone. It would no doubt be necessary to create the necessary institutional structures – this would be a condition which the UK could demand.

There might be a case for a type of European equivalent of the Buy American Act. Aircraft are a case in point. One of the main savings on long production runs is the spreading of the launching cost, i.e. R and D and jigging and tooling costs. Professor

1. There appears to be some difference as to the origins of this notion but the true parents, as opposed to foster parents, appear to be Swann and McLachlan (1967, pp. 39–40).

S. G. Sturmey (1964) has been able to show that, for an aircraft such as the BAC-111, total unit costs can fall by as much as a third as the production run lengthens from thirty to 100 aircraft. Clearly, this is of significance to Europe where the tendency is for aircraft to be produced for a small home market with the hope of a few foreign orders. Shirley Williams, writing in March 1966, pointed out that orders for the BAC-111, an aircraft proven in service, then stood at ninety, many supplied, plus twenty-one options, whereas in the case of the Douglas DC-9, which was similar in type but had only just entered service, the order book was four times as long (Williams, 1966). Clearly, if European Governments and airlines could collaborate they could tip the balance in the Community's favour in world markets. The subject of aircraft suggests that in arms procurement, too, much could be gained by common specifications.

It can be argued that this close collaboration is necessary if UK and European industry is to be prevented from falling into US hands. Already in the UK one tenth of manufacturing industry is American-owned. It has been pointed out that if current trends continue the figure will be 25 per cent by 1981 (Dunning, 1969). The problem becomes particularly acute when concentration of foreign ownership occurs in industries of strategic significance. From a technological point of view it is questionable whether the nation states of Western Europe are viable any longer. Today they face the American challenge. Tomorrow there may be others.

It is clear that part of the advantage of entry into the EEC resides in the development of positive integration policies as opposed to the merely negative measures involving the removal of discriminations in tariffs and other fields. Critics can, of course, point to the fact that whereas negative integration is relatively easy and has indeed already been accomplished, positive integration is more difficult, requires the political will and is in large measure as yet a hope rather than a reality.

One of the oldest arguments for British entry is the competitive stimulus it would give to British industry. Of course the UK could unilaterally administer the necessary jolt by reducing import duties but that would not carry with it any compensating access to other national markets. Within a union the stimulus is assumed to emanate from two sources. One is structural – in concentrated industries the national monopoly becomes a Community oligopoly and in oligopolistic industries there is a diminution of oligopolistic collusion and awareness. The other is behavioural – within national markets there is a resistance to the idea of trespassing on the preserves of compatriots. This is less likely to be an inhibiting factor in foreign markets. In short, within the UK market a larger number of firms are likely to be contending for a market share and the foreign contenders are less likely to be inhibited than national ones. Two objections can be raised to this analysis. It is based on Scitovsky's analysis of Western European markets in the 1950s. These were characterized by a lack of anti-trust activity. The UK, on the other hand, has since 1956 been operating a Restrictive Practices Act which has undoubtedly had a stimulating effect on competition. The rigid system of cartels which the Monopolies Commission discovered between 1948 and 1956 is a thing of the past. The other point is that merely opening up national markets will not increase competition if the potential competitors have decided to keep out of each other's way. In this respect it is worth noting that a number of Monopolies Commission reports have revealed the existence of international quota and price agreements involving UK and EEC firms.

There are of course other factors which have not been taken into account. The UK obviously has an interest in buoyant world trade and this in turn requires an ample and expanding supply of world liquidity. The Six for their part exercise a very considerable influence in international monetary matters. For example, at the Rio De Janiero IMF Conference in 1967, it was decided that important decisions regarding the international monetary system would require a majority of 85 per cent. Provided the Six can maintain their unity this will confer upon them a very considerable influence. From this point of view membership of an enlarged Community would enable the UK to exercise an important influence in matters such as the policy on SDRs. But there is more to it than this. It seems possible that the Six may eventually proceed to create a common currency via a common currency policy and a European unit of account. Equally, in the international monetary sphere the possibility exists that the Common Market could create a European reserve unit which The *Economist* has chosen to call the Europa. This would provide the world with an alternative to the Dollar as a medium for reserves. The Dollar and Europa might in the longer term be replaced by a fully international system based on an IMF unit. In so far as the Six have interests in this sphere, membership might provide the basis for a solution to the sterling balance problem through the agency of a Europe-backed funding operation. If part of an agreement on enlarging the Community consisted of a genuine expression of willingness to find a permanent solution to the sterling balance problem then indeed membership would appear a good deal more attractive in economic terms.

So far the discussion has centred on the advantages of entry. An alternative way of looking at the subject is to consider what might happen if the UK were not to join. It has been argued that if the UK industry had to continue to face the common external tariff then it would be driven to seek ways around it and one would be to set up subsidiaries within the EEC – which would involve a loss of investment and job opportunities. This may be a correct assessment of what would happen. But equally EEC industry would presumably be forced to set up in the UK. The balance might therefore be even. There are, however, a number of doubts surrounding the counter-balancing flow from the EEC. British industry might be attracted by the large tariff-free EEC market and the opportunities it presents to exploit scale economies. But would the UK offer the same opportunities? The answer is probably No. It is true that there would be access to the other EFTA economies but these are not geographically contiguous. But there is more to it than that. If a new plant is established in a market it will have to be of optimum scale in order to be competitive. But it is also necessary that it be used to full capacity. In the EEC the probability of the latter condition being fulfilled is the greatest, and there are two reasons for this. Firstly, the size of the market is greater and therefore, with a given growth rate, the extra annual increment of demand is greater. Secondly, in recent years the EEC growth rate has been faster than that of the UK. This suggests that investment in the EEC would be more attractive. Even if the UK capital outflow did not increase (for reasons referred to above) it can be argued that US capital might increasingly prefer the EEC.

What then does all this amount to? It indicates that entry would entail a significant cost. (This cost is, of course, to a large extent calculated on the basis of the existing financial rules of the common agricultural policy.) But there are advantages of membership although these are either less easily quantifiable or are attended by uncertainty. Because of this it would be a mistake to overestimate them. It is also worth stressing that many of the possible advantages – for example, in the fields of international money and advanced technology – will require that significant steps be taken in the institutional field. If Britain seeks to minimize her political commitment she may also minimize her economic advantages. The matter may therefore be summarized thus. Economic, as opposed to political, arguments indicate that there is a case for negotiation but not for merely signing on the dotted line. It would also be a mistake to assume that ultimately the economic case for entry can be treated in isolation from considerations of the future political and institutional structure of Europe.

This discussion of the pros and cons ignores the other important problem which is that even if the economic case for UK membership was without spot or blemish it might be vetoed. Although political factors must be extremely influential in determining the attitude of the Six both collectively and individually, economic factors cannot be ignored. The French objections in 1967 were that the UK had a substantial balance-of-payments deficit and that the sterling liabilities would be an embarrassment to the Six. Progress on the membership issue may therefore depend upon the achievements recorded in dealing with these twin objections. At the time of writing the UK has achieved a substantial balance-of-payments surplus. The switch in emphasis towards the vigorous application of monetary policy and away from incomes policies, as well as the imposition of a ceiling on Government spending, indicate at long last a growing realism in British economic policy. On the side of sterling it can be argued that the Basle Facility and the Sterling Area Agreements have altered the situation radically. On the other hand, as Professor H. G. Johnson has pointed out,

... the arrangements do leave open the question whether the ultimate intention is to fund the official sterling area balance into some new and more reliable international asset such as Special Drawing Rights, which many experts have recommended, or to restore them to their original freely disposable status, once Britain has put her balance of payments on a sound footing, as one suspects is the hope of the Bank of England. To the extent that the suspicion remains that Britain still hankers to maintain a reserve currency role, there is a continuing foundation for European doubts about the desirability of admitting her to membership in the EEC, at least unless and until her balance-of-payments position has been strengthened enough to make the international role of sterling an asset and not a liability (Johnson, 1969, p. 29).

Although space does not permit a review of the present tactical position, it might be noted that the devaluation of the Franc indicates that the common agricultural policy rules are not immutable and a French holier-than-thou attitude on the UK payments position is somewhat less likely.

The Alternative

Some people do, however, point to an alternative to EEC membership in the form of a North Atlantic Free Trade Area (NAFTA). The geographical scope of such an arrangement can be said to be the EFTA, plus the US and Canada with the possible membership of Australia, New Zealand and Japan. A study by Maxwell Stamp Associates has attempted to assess the increasing trade resulting from British membership of NAFTA and of the EEC. In this anlaysis the NAFTA partners are assumed to be the US and Canada. The results are shown in Table 6.

The export increase (trade creation) represents the results of tariff disarmament in respect of UK goods by the North American partners. The export increase (trade diversion) is derived from the fact that tariff disarmament would not extend to the EEC and therefore the UK would gain at its expense. The import increase would be the effect of the UK disarming against its North Atlantic partners. If Japan joined, the export increase (trade diversion) would fall by £248 million whilst direct trade between the UK and Japan would cancel out. Thus the trade balance

Table 6

Increasing Trade Resulting from UK Membership of NAFTA and of EEC (U.S. $ Million)

	NAFTA	EEC
Export increase (trade diversion)	292	316
Export increase (trade creation)	552	191
Import increase	189	286
Net change	655	221

Source: Maxwell Stamp Associates (1967), p. 46.

would improve by £407 million compared with £221 million if the UK joined the EEC. All these calculations pre-date the November 1967 devaluation. Other advantages are adduced. Because it will be a free trade area links with the Commonwealth could be retained. However, these preferences would be eroded if New Zealand and Australia, and other Commonwealth countries, joined in the arrangement. Other advantages have been claimed such as the economies of scale and increased specialization in a large dynamic market which would include the richest countries in the world in terms of *per capita* income. Then there would be a stimulating force of increased competition as well as an increased infusion of American capital, technology and managerial 'know-how'. There is also evidence to suggest that in terms of economic growth the US and Canada will outpace the EEC in the next decade or so.

Sceptics would no doubt raise the following objections. The Common Market exists whereas the NAFTA is an idea which has not yet been raised at inter-governmental level in the way in which British Common Market membership has. Is there at the highest level a political will to create such an arrangement? Does the behaviour of US industry, particularly in the light of experience in the Kennedy Round in respect of chemicals, lead to the expectation that total tariff disarmament is a realistic prospect? John Pinder and Roy Pryce also doubt the calculations of Stamp and Cowie and make this observation:

Stamp and Cowie say that 'The lowering of the tariff barriers between

Japan and the UK would lead to an almost equal increase in trade both ways'. But they have no right to be so confident; the effects of free trade with an economy that is moving as fast as Japan's with a growth rate of about 10 per cent a year, are quite unpredictable (Pinder and Pryce, 1969, p. 81).

They also raise the point that whereas competition within an enlarged EEC would be between equals, the NAFTA would involve competition between economies of distinctly different levels of wealth, technical ability and capital intensity. They observe:

The general picture is that Britain's labour-intensive traditional industries do well while its modern ones do badly. One does not need an over-heated imagination to fear that a large section of the UK economy could be relegated permanently to the more backward industries, while our skilled and enterprising people, together with as much of our capital as can do so, move to America where the modern industries and the future lie (Pinder and Pryce, 1969, p. 84).

Common Commercial Policy

Although a common commercial policy embraces a variety of subjects, clearly the most important is the level of the common external tariff. Since the tariff is the distinguishing feature of a customs union, and is the aspect of the Common Market which touches so many of the leading trading countries in the world, it is fitting that the negotiations concerning its size should be the final topic for consideration in this book.

The Rome Treaty confers upon the Commission the specific responsibility of conducting tariff negotiations with third countries. In 1960 the Six had to present to the GATT the common tariff which was to replace the tariffs of France, West Germany, Italy and the Benelux. The GATT rules require that the average incidence of the common tariff be no greater than the average incidence of the tariffs it replaces. In practice the common level was 8·2 per cent which was less than the 9·3 per cent of the tariffs it replaced. As a result the majority of the contracting parties to the GATT were satisfied. Furthermore, in anticipation of the Dillon Round of tariff negotiations (named after Douglas Dillon the then US Under-Secretary of State), the Community decided provisionally to reduce the new tariff by 20 per cent. As a result, national tariffs were initially aligned on the original tariff less 20 per cent, except where smaller cuts were negotiated and consolidated in the Dillon Round.

In July 1962 the late President Kennedy, speaking in Philadelphia, made his Declaration of Interdependence. This foreshadowed a US policy of North Atlantic free trade and partnership with a united Europe on terms of equality. The Trade Expansion Act of 1962 gave concrete expression to these aspirations. It conferred a negotiating mandate to establish full free trade in goods where the US and the EEC together accounted for 80 per cent of free world trade. Otherwise only a 50 per cent across-the-board cut could be negotiated. In practice the failure of the UK to join the EEC meant that full free trade was ruled out of the ensuing Kennedy Round. Negotiations proper opened in Geneva in May 1964 and were concluded in May 1967.

Although the participants failed to achieve all their objectives, substantial progress was made. A number of difficulties had stood in the way of a successful outcome. One was the fact that the US Congress insisted that agriculture be included in the negotiations. This was partly necessary in order to secure the successful passage of the Act, but it was also justified by the fact that US sales of agricultural products to the Community constituted $1600 million of the $5500 million total sales thereto. The agricultural negotiations were also complicated by the somewhat protectionist tendency in the Community's agricultural policy together with the fact that, partly as a result of the French withdrawal, the financial rules and the common prices for products other than grain were not agreed until quite late on.

Another problem was the issue of excluding altogether some products from the tariff-cutting and applying cuts of less than 50 per cent in the case of others. In particular, there was the problem of how to deal with the disparity problem where, for example, US tariffs were so much higher than those of the Six and a straight 50 per cent cut would be unacceptable. The main sticking point came in the case of chemicals. The Six, backed by the UK and the Swiss, were anxious to have the American Selling Price (ASP) system abolished. Under this arrangement the price upon which

US import duties were applied was not the European export price but the price at which comparable goods were produced in the US. This resulted in duties of up to 170 per cent *ad valorem*. The system also applied to other products such as rubber shoes.

The outcome of the negotiations was as follows. Although many cuts of 50 per cent were agreed, and the number of products excluded from tariff-cutting altogether or subject to cuts of less than 50 per cent was greatly reduced, the average cut was only about 35 per cent. The total value of international trade affected was $40,000 million per annum, that is to say, about one quarter of free world trade. In respect of chemicals, the US accepted that should the ASP system be abolished, irrespective of whether products were subject to it, duties would be reduced by 50 per cent and down to a ceiling of 20 per cent (except in special cases). The Community for its part undertook to reduce its duties by 50 per cent (subject to exceptions). If the ASP system was not abolished,[1] the US would reduce by 50 per cent its duties in excess of 8 per cent and by 20 per cent those below that rate. The Community would then only reduce by 20 per cent duties below 25 per cent and by 30 per cent those above that figure.

In the agricultural sector the Kennedy Round fell far short of the hopes entertained by the US and the Six. The Community argued for a system of international discipline and commitments about the levels of national support for farmers. But in the event these were dropped. All that emerged was an increased minimum world price for wheat of $1·73 per bushel[2] and an agreement to give 'food aid' to needy countries. This was to consist of 4·5 million tons of grain a year. The US was to finance 42 per cent of the cost, the EEC 23 per cent, Canada 11 per cent and the UK and Australia 5 per cent each.

The significance of the Kennedy Round should not, however, be underestimated. Not only did the result enhance the status of the Commission but it also showed that the Six could negotiate as a single unit with the rest of the world on vital matters. The

1. It now seems improbable that it will be abolished.
2. This was a concession to the US which had looked for greater access to the EEC agricultural market. By the middle of 1969 there were signs that the agreement to keep the price level above the minimum had been breached.

progressive reduction of duties will provide the participating economies with a stimulus similar to that felt internally by the Six. This experience also provides the UK with a preparatory taste of what full Community membership is like.

References

BALASSA, B. (1962), *The Theory of Economic Integration*, Allen & Unwin, p. 224.

BEEVER, R. C. (1969), *Trade Unions and Free Labour Movement in the E.E.C.*, PEP and Chatham House, pp. 27–8.

Britain and the European Communities: An Economic Assessment (1970), HMSO, Cmnd 4289.

BUTTERWICK, M., and ROLFE, E. N. (1968), 'How the common agricultural policy is financed', *European Community*, no. 11, p. 11.

COLLINS, D. (1966), 'Towards a European social policy', *Journal of Common Market Studies*, vol. 5, no. 1, pp. 42–3.

CONFEDERATION OF BRITISH INDUSTRIES (1966), *Britain and Europe*, vol. 2: *An Industrial Reappraisal*, CBI.

DAHLBERG, K. A. (1968), 'The EEC Commission and the politics of the free movement of labour', *Journal of Common Market Studies*, vol. 6, no. 3, pp. 310–33.

DUNNING, J. H. (1969), *The Role of American Investment in the British Economy*, PEP, p. 124.

EUROPEAN COAL AND STEEL COMMUNITY HIGH AUTHORITY (1967), *Europe and Energy*, ECSC.

EEC COMMISSION (1961), *Memorandum on the General Lines of the Common Transport Policy*, EEC.

EEC COMMISSION (1962), *Programme for Implementation of the Common Transport Policy*, EEC.

EEC COMMISSION (1965), 'Options de la politique tarifaire dans les transport', *Etudes Serie Transport*, no. 1, esp. ch. 32.

EEC COMMISSION (1967), *First General Report on the Activities of the Communities*, EEC.

EEC COMMISSION (1968a), 'First guide lines for a Community energy policy', *Bulletin of the European Communities Supplement*, no. 12.

EEC COMMISSION (1968b), *Notice Concerning Agreements, Decisions and Concerted Practices in the Field of Co-operation between Enterprises*, EEC, p. 1.

EFTA (1966), *Building EFTA*, EFTA, p. 76.

EUROPEAN PARLIAMENT (1965), *Document 1, 1965/6 Session*, 22 March.

INTERNATIONAL LABOUR OFFICE (1956), *Social Aspects of European Economic Co-operation*, ILO.

JOHNSON, H. G. (1958), 'The gains from freer trade with Europe: an estimate', *Manchester School of Economic and Social Studies*, vol. 26, no. 3, p. 255.

JOHNSON, H. G. (1969), 'Financial and monetary problems: Britain and the EEC', in M. A. G. von Meerhaeghe (ed.), *Economics: Britain and the EEC*, Longmans.

KITZINGER, U. (1961), *The Challenge of the Common Market*, Blackwell, p. 38.

LAYTON, C. (1966), *Trans-Atlantic Investments*, Atlantic Institute, Table 17.

LEVI SANDRI, L. (1965). 'The contribution of regional action to the construction of Europe', *Third International Congress on Regional Economics*, Rome, p. 2.

LUNDGREN, N. (1969), 'Customs unions of industrialized West European countries', in G. R. Denton (ed.), *Economic Integration in Europe*, Weidenfeld & Nicolson, p. 52.

MANSFIELD, E. (1964), 'Industrial research and development expenditures', *Journal of Political Economy*, vol. 62, no. 4, pp. 337–8.

MAXWELL STAMP ASSOCIATES (1967), *The Free Trade Area Option*, Atlantic Trade Study.

MUSGRAVE, P. B. (1965), 'An evaluation of investment income taxation within the European Common Market', *Public Finance*, vol. 20, pp. pp. 248–95.

MUSSARD, R. (1962), 'The regulation of restrictive business practices under the Common Market Treaty', *International and Comparative Law Quarterly*, Supplementary Publication no. 4, p. 17.

OECD (1963), *Science, Economic Growth and Government Policy*, OECD, p. 87.

PALMER, M., LAMBERT, J., FORSYTH, M., MORRIS, A., and WOHLGEMUTH, E. (1968), *European Unity: A Survey of the European Organisations*, Allen & Unwin, p. 32.

PINDER, J., and PRYCE, R. (1969), *Europe after De Gaulle*, Penguin Books.

PISANI, E. (1969), *The Agricultural Problems Involved in British Membership of the Common Market*, Action Committee for the United States of Europe, p. 31.

PLOWDEN, E. N., and WINNACKER, K. (1969), *Techological Co-operation in a Community Enlarged by British Entry*, Action Committee for the United States of Europe.

SARACENO, P. (1965), *The Economic Development of the Mezzogiorno*, Giuffre, p. 4.

SCHMOOKLER, J. (1959), 'Bigness, fewness and research', *Journal of Political Economy*, vol. 117, no. 6, pp. 631–2.

SELECT COMMITTEE ON NATIONALISED INDUSTRIES (1963), *Report*, HMSO, vol. 3, pp. 284–5, 349.

SHEAHAN, J. (1963), *Promotion and Control of Industry in Post-War France*, Harvard University Press, p. 201.

STRANGE, S. (1967), *The Sterling Problem and the Six*, PEP and Chatham House, p. 5.

STURMEY, S. G. (1964), 'Cost curves and pricing in aircraft production', *Economic Journal*, vol. 74, no. 296, p. 969.

SWANN, D., and MCLACHLAN, D. L. (1967), *Concentration or Competition: A European Dilemma*, PEP and Chatham House.

WARLEY, T. K. (1967), *Agriculture: The Cost of Joining The Common Market*, PEP and Chatham House.

WARLEY, T. K. (1969), 'Economic integration of European agriculture', in G. R. Denton (ed.), *Economic Integration in Europe*, Weidenfeld & Nicolson, p. 304.

WILLIAMS, S. (1966), 'European unity and technological collaboration', *European Community*, no. 3, p. 8.

WORLEY, J. S. (1961), 'Industrial research and the new competition', *Journal of Political Economy*, vol. 69, no. 2, p. 135.

YANNOPOULOS, G. N. (1969), 'Economic integration and labour movements', in G. R. Denton (ed.), *Economic Integration in Europe*, Weidenfeld & Nicolson, p. 229.

Further Reading

Andel, N., 'Problems of harmonization of social security policies in a common market', in C. S. Shoup (ed.), *Fiscal Harmonization in Common Markets*, Columbia University Press, 1967, vol. 1.

Balassa, B., *The Theory of Economic Integration*, Allen & Unwin, 1962.

Barnes, W. G., *Europe and the Developing World*, P E P and Chatham House, 1967.

Barzanti, S., *The Underveloped Areas within the Common Market*, Princeton University Press, 1965.

Bayliss, B. T., *European Transport*, Mason, 1965.

Butterwick, M., and Rolfe, C. J., *Food, Farming and the Common Market*, Oxford University Press, 1968.

Camps, M., *Britain and the European Community 1955–1963*, Oxford University Press, 1964.

Carli, G., *On the Monetary Aspects of British Entry into the Common Market*, Action Committee for the United States of Europe, 1969.

Collins, D., 'Towards a European social policy', *Journal of Common Market Studies*, 1966, vol. 5, no. 1, pp. 26–48.

Confederation of British Industries, *Britain and Europe*, vol. 2: *An Industrial Reappraisal*, CBI, 1966.

Cosgrove, C. A., 'The E E C and developing countries', in G. R. Denton (ed.), *Economic Integration in Europe*, Weidenfeld & Nicolson, 1969.

Cox, R. W., 'Social and labour policy in the E E C', *British Journal of Industrial Relations*, 1963, vol. 1, no. 1, pp. 5–22.

Denton, G. R., *Planning in the E.E.C.: The Medium-Term Economic Policy Programme of the European Economic Community*, P E P and Chatham House, 1967.

Denton, G. R., 'Planning and integration: medium-term policy as an instrument of integration', in G. R. Denton (ed.), *Economic Integration in Europe*, Weidenfeld & Nicolson, 1969.

Dosser, D., and Han, S. S., *Taxes in the E E C and Britain: The Problems of Harmonization*, P E P and Chatham House, 1968.

E E C Commission, *The Development of a European Capital Market* (The Segré Report), E E C, 1966.

E E C Monetary Committee, *Reports on the Activities of the Monetary Committee*, E E C.

European Coal and Steel Community High Authority, *Europe and Energy*, E C S C, 1967.

European Parliamentary Assembly, *Report on Regional Policy in the E E C*, (The Birkelbach Report), E E C, 1963.

Federal Trust for Education and Research, *The European Capital Market*, FTER, 1967.

Frank, I., *The European Common Market*, Stevens, 1961.

Henderson, W. O., *The Genesis of the Common Market*, Cass, 1962.

Johnson, H. G., 'Financial and monetary problems: Britain and the EEC', in M. A. G. van Meerhaeghe (ed.), *Economics: Britain and the EEC*, Longmans, 1969.

Layton, C., *Trans-Atlantic Investments*, Atlantic Institute, 1966.

Layton, C., *European Advanced Technology: A Programme for Integration*, PEP and Allen & Unwin, 1969.

Liesner, H. H., 'Policy harmonization in the EEC and EFTA', in G. R. Denton (ed.), *Economic Integration in Europe*, Weidenfeld & Nicolson, 1969.

Lipsey, R. G., 'The theory of customs unions: a general survey',*Economic Journal*, 1960, vol. 70, pp. 496–513.

Maxwell Stamp Associates, *The Free Trade Area Option*, Atlantic Trade Study, 1967.

Mayne, R., *The Community of Europe*, Gollancz, 1962.

Mayne, R., *Institutions of the European Community*, PEP and Chatham House, 1968.

McCrone, G., 'Regional policy in the European communities', in G. R. Denton (ed.), *Economic Integration in Europe*, Weidenfeld & Nicolson, 1969.

McLachlan, D. L., and Swann, D., *Competition Policy in the European Communities*, Oxford University Press, 1967.

Meade, J., *The Theory of Customs Unions*, North-Holland Publishing Co., 1955.

Okibo, P. C. C., *Africa and the Common Market*, Longmans, 1967.

Palmer, M., Lambert, J., Forsyth, M., Morris, A., and Wohlgemuth, E., *European Unity: A Survey of the European Organizations*, Allen & Unwin, 1968.

Pinder, J., 'Advanced technology: Britain and the EEC', in M. A. G. van Meerhaeghe (ed.), *Economics: Britain and the EEC*, Longmans, 1969.

Pinder, J., and Pryce, R., *Europe after De Gaulle*, Penguin Books, 1969.

Pisani, E., *The Agricultural Problems Involved in British Membership of the Common Market*, Action Committee for the United States of Europe, 1969.

Plowden, E. N., and Winnacker, K., *Technological Co-operation in a Community Enlarged by British Entry*, Action Committee for the United States of Europe, 1969.

Robertson, D., *Scope for New Trade Strategy*, Atlantic Trade Study, 1968.

Schumacher, E. F., 'The struggle for a European energy policy', *Journal of Common Market Studies*, 1964, vol. 2.

Scitovsky, T., *Economic Theory and Western European Integration*, Allen & Unwin, 1958.

Servan-Schreiber, J.-J., *Le Défi Américain*, Denoel, 1967; translated as *The American Challenge*, Penguin Books, 1969.

Shoup, C. S. (ed.), *Fiscal Harmonization in Common Markets*, vols 1 and 2, Columbia University Press, 1967.

Strange, S., *The Sterling Problem and the Six*, PEP and Chatham House, 1967.

Swann, D., 'Cartels and concentrations – issues and progress', in G. R. Denton (ed.), *Economic Integration in Europe*, Weidenfeld & Nicolson, 1969.

Swann, D., and McLachlan, D. L., *Concentration or Competition? A European Dilemma*, PEP and Chatham House, 1967.

Triffin, R., *On the Monetary Aspects of the Accession of Great Britain to the Common Market*, Action Committee for the United States of Europe, 1969.

Van Meerhaeghe, M. A. G. 'Economics: Britain and the EEC – an introduction', in M. A. G. van Meerhaeghe (ed.), *Economics: Britain and the EEC*, Longmans, 1969.

Viner, J., *The Customs Union Issue*, Carnegie, 1950.

Warley, T. K., *Agriculture: The Cost of Joining the Common Market*, PEP and Chatham House, 1967.

Warley, T. K., 'Economic integration of European agriculture', in G. R. Denton (ed.), *Economic Integration in Europe*, Weidenfeld & Nicolson, 1969.

Yannopoulos, G. N., 'Economic integration and labour movements', in G. R. Denton (ed.), *Economic Integration in Europe*, Weidenfeld & Nicolson, 1969.

Index